"Wanted to give you an update. We have put in all of your stuff...we just went for it and have implemented most everything. We are 7-7 right now after an 0-4 start. We start 3 freshmen and 3 sophomores and I really feel that things are turning the corner here. Players seem to be buying in to all aspects of the program and seem rejuvenated by the new things we have implemented."

—Mike Swartzentruber
Martinsville High School

"Thanks for the info! I've been to the ABCA and the Wisconsin clinic since last season and have seen probably 25 DVDS. None of those sessions or DVDs has been more valuable to our WBCA clinic. Thanks again!"

—John Matera
Tremper High School

"After reading the article on your team in 'Collegiate Baseball' and more about your program's philosophy, I wrote down everything. Then I saw your Prezi, files, and videos through the site and purchased everything. Thank you for helping to improve the game and sharing your program. Winning streak or no winning streak, the perspective on the sport of baseball is what your players learn and take with them and that is what it is all about...1-Pitch Warrior for LIFE!"

—Kevin Connor
Oregon High School

"I heard you speak in Minneapolis last weekend and was very impressed with your knowledge and passion for our great game of baseball. I have been coaching at the same small school in southern Minnesota (New Richland) for 37 years and have tried to come up with a QAB assessment chart for years, and yours seems very thorough."

—Jeff Reese
New Richland High School

"1-Pitch Warrior is awesome. I have implemented this program and it allows us to consistently play our best. I thank you for putting this program together and sharing it with others.'

—Jeremy Richey
Seymour High School

"The 1-Pitch Warrior blew me away. It was exactly what I was looking for. I was extremely impressed with the simplicity of things, and loved how it gives ways to implement the strategies."

—Aaron Zweifel
Badger High School

"I'm always looking for the best speakers in the country to put in front of our eager group of high school, college, and youth coaches. Last February, Justin Dehmer did an outstanding job with the 1-Pitch Warrior System. The 1-Pitch Warrior was the highlight of the clinic. I highly recommend Justin to any clinic trying to put great information in front of their coaches."

—Mark Fuller
WHSBCA Clinic Director

1-PITCH WARRIOR SERIES

MENTAL TOUGHNESS TRAINING SYSTEM

JUSTIN B. DEHMER
1-Pitch Warrior, LLC

Visit www.1pitchwarrior.com/extras
for BONUS 1-Pitch Warrior Tips
& FREE Systems of Success

www.1pitchwarrior.com
Twitter: @1pitchwarrior
www.facebook.com/1pitchwarrior

Justin Dehmer
1-Pitch Warrior
1-Pitch Warrior Publishing
1-Pitch Warrior, LLC

1-Pitch Warrior
Mental Toughness Training System
A 1-Pitch Warrior Series Book

Printed in the United States of America
Edited by: Cristine Hammer and Carole Henning
Cover Design and Layout: David Brizendine
Illustrations: Justin Dehmer
Photography: Ryan Riley

Justin B. Dehmer
1-Pitch Warrior
Mental Toughness Training System
A 1-Pitch Warrior Series Book
Justin B. Dehmer

ISBN: 9780615707174

PREFACE

1-Pitch Warrior – Guide to Mental Toughness is the key to unlocking your full potential as a player or a coach. The principles provided in this book will not only allow you to find your true potential on the field, but I am also confident that they will enrich your life off the field, as well. Being a 1-Pitch Warrior is much more than winning on the baseball field; it is about winning the day, making the most of opportunities—good or bad— that come your way. It's about learning how to respond to adversity and handle anything that baseball—or life—throws at you.

With this book you will learn many systems of success, including the 5 Ps of Primetime Programs. Playing for the present and trying to win each pitch is broken down in great detail so you will actually learn a cyclical process by which you can ensure that you're playing the game as a 1-Pitch Warrior. You will learn about measuring performance on skills and strategies that have meaning, and that matter far more than just the basics like averages, RBIs, wins, etc. Topics will include: B.A.S.E.2., A3P, Quality At-Bats, Quality Innings, and others.

The last part of my book is devoted to developing a vocabulary among your coaching staff and players so that you all use the same language in defining what it means to be a 1-Pitch Warrior. These terms can be discussed at practice or assigned as daily reading for your players before practice.

Whether you are a veteran coach seeking that first state title, or a high school player trying to make the varsity, there is something for everyone in this book. The 1-Pitch Warrior Mentality is for anyone who wants to attack life and live in the moment. Remember that the past is history, the future is a mystery; we call it the "present" because it is a gift. Here's to unwrapping the moments in life that you desire but have yet to experience. Good luck on your journey as a 1-Pitch Warrior!

www.1pitchwarrior.com

DEDICATION

This book is dedicated to my parents, John and JoAnn Dehmer. You taught me that nothing was out of reach as long as I truly believed it could be accomplished, and if I worked with a tenacity that was unmatched by others. You watched my love of the game develop over the years, from player to coach, and have been my biggest fans, no matter what. You invested countless hours and precious dollars helping me practice, watching my games, going to camps, and helping our program. All of it was done out of love. I cannot repay what you have done for me. I thank you for all the love and support you have shown me, through disappointments and triumphs. I have been blessed with great parents and I will continue the lessons you taught me with my own children, giving them everything they need to be successful at whatever passions they pursue in life.

ACKNOWLEDGMENTS

To my family: Angie, Grace, and Gavin. I know that being the head coach's family is never easy. Saying I appreciate all you have done for me just doesn't cut it. As far as I am concerned, you are the MVPs—my Most Valuable People. It is hard to describe what this journey has meant to me and knowing that you have been apart of it makes it that much more special. Thank you for everything. I love you. Forever. I promise.

It is with immense gratitude that I thank the players, coaches, and families that have been a part of my coaching career. You have all been a special part of my life and have strenthened my passion for baseball. Thank you for your support and for helping make the impossible possible.

I must acknowledge the many coaches I have had over the years. You all helped shape my thinking and knowledge of the game. Special thanks to a few standout coaches who were extra special along the way: Jay "The Himel" Himelstein, for always believing in me and giving me the opportunity to take countless swings in his cage on Rose Lane where my pursuit of excellence really started; Coach Clint Myers, for being an unrelenting but understanding coach who never expected anything less than excellence; Coach Jon Wente, for showing me what quiet leadership was all about; Coach Mike Treadwell, for always being able to talk with me even when no one else would; and Scout John Kazanas for always going the extra mile for me and teaching me the game I so dearly love.

I have to thank my assistant coaches over the years—Jordan

Loebig, John Loebig, Jon Fitzpatrick, Sean Smith, and Justin Stoulil—for believing in me and the 1-Pitch Warrior Mentality System. Thank you for all the time you have spent with the players and me. I have loved every minute of it.

I also have to give a huge thanks to Brian Cain for playing an instrumental part in my coaching style, in our team's success, and for the encouragement to tell our story through speaking and writing this book. I can truly say that I have learned from the best and he is the Master of The Mental Game. Thank you for your guiding light!

I would not feel right without mentioning my faith in the Lord, Jesus Christ. I know that through God all things are possible!

CONTENTS

FORWARD

88 wins…in a row!

Most people don't brush their teeth 88 straight days in a row, let alone win 88 straight high school baseball games and 3 straight state championships.

I have worked with high school and NCAA national championship winning programs. Worked as the mental conditioning coach for the Washington Nationals and had over 360 players drafted in the last ten years, including over 20 first-round picks.

Coach Dehmer was able to put a mental conditioning system together for his players that helped unlock their potential and play their best when it means the most.

When you read this book, you will see a lot of the same terminology used in my books *Toilets, Bricks, Fish Hooks and PRIDE: The Peak Performance Toolbox EXPOSED* (www.toiletsbricksfishhooksandpride.com), *So What, Next Pitch!: How To Play Your Best When It Means The Most* (www.sowhatnextpitch.com) and *The Mental Conditioning Manual: Your Blueprint For Excellence* (www.thementalconditioningmanual.com).

The reason why the terminology and examples will sound familiar is because Coach Dehmer USES the mental game and has taken it to another level with his program. As one of the top baseball coaches in the country, he understands how to put the system in place and has taken ownership of the material because he uses it every day in his teaching, on the field, and in his life.

Justin and Martensdale-St. Mary's set the standard for

consistency and excellence in high school baseball. The 1-Pitch Warrior Mentality that Dehmer's players were taught is revealed to you in this book.

He has simplified the mental game and includes statistical ways to reinforce to your players the process of winning and also provides the framework for the 1-Pitch Warrior Mentality.

Coach Dehmer has given the baseball community an open look into excellence and what it means to play your best when it matters most. Any coach, player, or parent who has not read 1-Pitch Warrior is missing out on a great opportunity to improve their game and take it to the next level. Coach Dehmer is a mental assassin in training and a master of the mental game.

Brian Cain

Mental Conditioning Coach

www.BrianCain.com

INTRODUCTION

Eighty-Eight wins in a row. To this day, I have a hard time believing that we actually won that many consecutive games. With all the errors that baseball can bring on a nightly basis—an opposing pitcher who is lights out on the mound, defensive miscues, mental mistakes, bats that have gone cold, coaching mistakes, and any number of other facets that come with coaching high school players and the subtleties of baseball—we were able to overcome all of these things for 88 straight games and win three straight state titles from 2010 to 2012, too. You will hear me say it time and time again, that we were not perfect...ever. It is plain that we do not preach perfection in our program; what we do preach is knowing that adversity will come our way in many forms throughout the season and that, no matter what the situation, we must be able to handle that and yet still strive for excellence in all we do. In every game, there was good and bad. What we did better than our opponents was, not only prepare for success, but also plan for failure. We played the game as 1-Pitch Warriors, which became our motto throughout our winning streak and even after it was over.

As we continued our streak from 43 wins in a row in 2010, to 44 more consecutive wins in 2011, and 1 more in 2012, it became very clear to me that this phenomenon was much more about the way we prepared for each night than simply having great players. There is no doubt that we were a very talented team and talent doesn't hurt when it comes to winning games. But talent alone does not, and never will mean certain victory. To win 88 times in a row, through three consecutive state titles, with a schedule that demanded focus night in and night out, had to be the result of much more than just physical skill and luck.

We played almost every night, starting the last week of May and continuing through the 4th of July week until the postseason started in the second week of July. We prepared relentlessly on the field—hitting, fielding, throwing, pitching, running the bases, etc. All the fundamentals were covered, but what I feel took us to the next level and allowed for the wins and titles was our mental approach to the game. During the 2010, 2011, and 2012 seasons, we became 1-Pitch Warriors and my players will always have that mentality as long as I coach. I feel it is the only way to play the game with consistency and to play your best when you need it most.

This book is designed to give you the insight into the things we discussed throughout the seasons leading up to, and during "The Streak." It will also give you insight into other philosophies and ways we measure the performance of our players that you will be able to use immediately in your program as a daily curriculum, mental minute, practice starter, skull session, etc. Make it your own and start helping your team develop the 1-Pitch Warrior Mentality today!

CHAPTER 1: HISTORY IN THE MAKING

Dehmer Shares Mental Strategies Used During Nation's Longest Winning Streak

This interview is between Brian Cain and Justin Dehmer, the head baseball coach at Martensdale-St. Mary's High School in Iowa. At the time of the interview, Coach Dehmer and his team were riding an eighty-game (80) winning streak. Since the time of this interview, the team ran its record to an all-time record of 87 games, which was topped a year later by Portsmouth High School in New Hampshire, who pushed it to 89 in a row. Martensdale-St. Mary's was able to win 88 consecutive games and ultimately ended up losing what would have been the record-tying game.

Coach Dehmer had his team focused not on eighty straight wins, nor on the national record. The team was not focused on its third straight state championship. Rather, Coach Dehmer focused his team on going 1 pitch at a time. Even after the streak was snapped, the focus and mentality never changed.

COACH DEHMER'S BACKGROUND

Brian Cain: Could you give a little bit of your background into how you got to where you are today as the Martensdale-St. Mary's head coach?

Justin Dehmer: I'm from Phoenix, Arizona. I grew up playing high school baseball at a big 5-A school there and then went on to Central Arizona where my head coach was Clint Myers, who is now the head women's softball coach at Arizona State. Coach Myers and the Sun Devils have had great success and won National Championships in 2008 and 2011. I went from

Central Arizona to Kansas State University and played there for a year. During that year I broke my finger.

I ended up getting a medical redshirt for that whole season. I went back to Arizona for two years, where I finished up at Grand Canyon University, got my teaching degree, and got a chance to play a couple more years of baseball before finishing off my career.

Then my wife, whom I met at Kansas State, and I decided to move back to Iowa, start a family, and put down some roots, and that's how I ended up in the great state of Iowa. My wife and her family are from Iowa and we just thought this would be a great place to raise a family.

I was teaching at Earlham High School, a small 1-A school, as the junior varsity and assistant varsity coach for a couple of years and had some success. Then, Martensdale-St. Mary's had a job open up. It had great tradition; a lot of state tournament appearances. It's one of those places where baseball is in the culture and taken very seriously.

My first two years as head coach, we were 19-11 (2008) and then 25-11 (2009). In 2010, we went 43-0, and right now (2011), we are currently 37-0.

ABOUT MARTENSDALE - ST. MARY'S

BC: Talk a little bit about St. Mary's. When some coaches see the title "St. Mary's," they will immediately think it's a school with a religious affiliation, and maybe a school that can recruit because it's a small private school. Is that the case?

JD: It's a public school. St. Mary's is a tiny, tiny town. If you drive through it and blink, you're going to miss it. The first thing you see when you come into St. Mary's is the baseball field and a gym in the outfield—that's our indoor facility with some batting cages.

The school itself happens to be in Martensdale; but the baseball field is in St. Mary's. The two towns joined up; it happens a lot here in Iow,a where you have towns combining to have a school and a school district. A lot of people look at our school name and think we're a private school. We are public. In 2010, we played Remsen St. Mary's, a private school, in the championship game, so there was a big confusion amongst everybody thinking that we both were private schools playing for the public school state title.

BC: How many students attend your school?

JD: I think the senior class this year was forty-two or forty-five. It's a small school. 1-A is as small as you can get in Iowa, and that is small. But, we have a lot of good baseball tradition. Some families have moved into our district, and we take some heat for that, but when you do things right and are successful, people want to be a part of what you're doing.

SUCCESSFUL HIGH SCHOOL COACHES GET RECRUITING RAP

BC: I see a lot of successful high school coaches getting that label of being recruiters, but high school kids and parents aren't idiots (well… some of them are). They want their kid to play at the next level. They're going to move into the town so they can go to the school that has the best coach, the best system for development, and does things the right way. There are a lot of coaches who do things right and get the recruiting card played on them.

You've established Martensdale-St. Mary's as a program that's doing great things for people who have a passion for baseball. It sounds like people who want to have a great experience can't pay to come to your school, but they can move into your district and be a part of that?

JD: Correct. I tell kids the story about when we went to the Junior College World Series at Central Arizona. Every single guy on our team went on to play at a 4-year school. Some of those guys got only one inning of pitching experience that year. They still went on to play somewhere, and that's kind of how we phrase it, too: If we have success as a team, then you as an individual are going to get looks, and you're probably going to get an opportunity to play at the next level. Three of our four seniors went on to play last year. We have only two seniors this year and they're definitely going to go somewhere. We've built a place where kids can come in, get better for four years and then go on and play somewhere else.

THE SYSTEM FOR SUCCESS

BC: Talk a little bit about your system. More exciting than the winning streak to me is the way you've done it. Can you talk about your process from a mental-game standpoint, where you got your system of teaching the mental game, and some of the things you brought to Martensdale-St. Mary's?

JD: In my playing experience, I was definitely NOT a master of the mental game in any way, shape, or form. I was probably one of the worst. I would beat myself up after a bad performance till no end. When I became a coach, I was going to have to be really, really good at teaching kids how to manage their heads, and making sure they gave themselves the best chance to succeed on a consistent basis. I was a very inconsistent player— always up and down. One night I'd be hot and the next time I'd be 0-for-4.

I had a pretty good grasp of the Xs and Os and how to treat kids, but I wanted to grab onto something that was worthwhile and made sense to me. Brian, a lot of what you use in the mental game and all of your terminology, the mental bricks, it just stuck with me and it clicked. I was just amazed. I couldn't get enough of it and I just kept feeding it to our kids.

Our big thing was the Five Ps of Peak Performance—to live in the Present moment, focus on the Process, stay Positive, have a champion's Perspective, and Prepare to the best of your ability. We try to play the game the way it's supposed to be played, which is pitch-by-pitch.

It sounds simple but getting kids to actually understand it, to have a routine and a process to go through— getting a deep breath, refocusing on some sort of focal point, and getting back into the present—takes time to develop. The mental game is something that they have to practice and work on. We make them write down their routine and how they are going to prepare for when adversity hits so that we all know ahead of time. I can almost tell you when guys are going to get a hit when they get into the box. When I see them take that big deep breath, I can tell when guys are locked in and in the present moment.

We also work a lot on our players' perspective. We try to teach our players that baseball is just a game; this is not life or death and there are bigger and more important things out there than this game. We're just going to enjoy it now and stay positive.

We also emphasize being a good teammate and sticking with a focus on the process instead of the outcome. That has been huge for us. We keep statistics, but statistics aren't important to me, or the team. The most important things are what we call quality pitches and quality at-bats. We keep track of those on a player-by-player basis. If the hitter moves a runner up with no outs, then that's a quality at-bat. There's nothing wrong with that. That's helping the team succeed; instead of an 0-for-1 that's a 1-for-1 in that kid's mind. He did his job. He moved the runner over, now we have a chance to score a run. The process is something that we really hammer home. It's all about committing to what we do on a daily basis and having quality practices.

We've had some great success with this approach. Our varsity has been amazing, but in the four years I've been there, our JV has lost only five games. There is a definite trickle-down effect. Our JV players are doing the same thing our varsity kids are doing, and when it's their turn to step in, it's a comfort factor and they know exactly what's going on.

Quality practice and quality preparation is a big one for us. I have to say we run some pretty long practices, but we run some pretty good ones, and we put a lot of time into preparing them. I think that's one of the biggest reasons why we have been successful; our players are getting better all the time.

ESTABLISH A PROGRAM 9-12

BC: You talked about getting your JV and varsity players together. How much of practice is spent together with JV and varsity?

JD: We're a small school. This year we have big numbers—twenty-eight kids between the JV and varsity. But in years past, we were right around twenty. Our JV team practices with our varsity, so they're really getting four years of the same coaching. When they come in as freshmen, we use the same terminology and language for four years. Flushing the mental brick, playing it one-pitch-at-a-time—they hear it daily for four years. That is really one of the reasons I enjoy coaching at a small school.

When you coach at a bigger, 4-A program, you don't get to see those kids for all four years. You hope your other coaches are doing the same thing, but that's not always the case. I know what's going on with my JV and even our seventh- and eighth-grade teams. They're doing the same stuff we are, so it's all the way through our program. It's a huge part of our culture and our success.

PRACTICE PHILOSOPHY

BC: Let's shift gears here for a bit. Can you talk about your practice philosophy? I think a lot of coaches think, "Okay, right now we're working on the mental game and then we're going to work on the physical game." Do you see working on the mental and physical game as something that you do together? Or are they separate?

JD: I see them as one and the same. When we're allowed to practice with our pitchers and catchers before practice officially starts in May, we'll start mentioning the mental game to them then.

We'll have a ten- or fifteen-minute session when we're breaking down the mental game and reviewing things they have read or seen in videos. Once we start practice and we're on the field in a live situation, coaching the mental game is more of an on-the-fly thing, where guys will turn to each other and say, "Hey, flush it, man." They literally will say that to each other during practices and games, and they'll get each other back on the same page, playing with a "so what, next pitch" mentality.

It's an atmosphere of excellence that we've created and it kind of runs itself, really. There are times when we as coaches will pull guys aside and say, "Hey, we got a lot of game left; let's get rid of that inning. Let's go back out there on the mound next inning— go one-pitch-at-a- time, and flush it. It wasn't great, but we can do better and let's not let that hamper our future here." And, it's pretty cool to see how it has all evolved and taken on a life of its own.

PLAYERS MUST TAKE OWNERSHIP

BC: It sounds like the ownership is with the players and their belief in the system is pretty solid.

JD: 100%. We have media coverage around the streak and when our guys get interviewed, I'll watch it on TV. Our guys are using the language, saying things like, "Yeah, we just play it one-pitch-at-a-time and we're not going to worry about what happened in the past or what's going to happen in the future. We're locked in on today and trying to get better today." It's pretty cool to see guys interviewed saying basically the same thing you've been saying for four years about how we want to approach the game and play it.

We're a physically talented team, but I've always said we want to be better mentally than we are physically. If we're better mentally than we are physically, then we're going to win a lot more games than we lose. The players have bought into it and they have no doubt that it's the reason for our eighty wins in a row.

We've fought in some pretty close one-run games, come-back games, games when we've really had to play one-pitch-at-a-time. We would continue to grind it out and play that way while the other team, maybe for only one inning, takes a lapse. We turn a walk, or one error, into two or three runs and all of a sudden we have the momentum, and we're ahead. Sticking with the process and playing pitch-to-pitch has been the reason for our success; there's no doubt about that.

1-PITCH WARRIORS

BC: One of the things that you've talked about in the media is this idea of being a "1-pitch warrior." What is a 1-pitch warrior?

JD: A 1-pitch warrior is a guy who plays the game one- pitch-at-a-time and knows how to do that even when something bad happens. He has the ability to move on to the next pitch. It may not be immediately, but whether it's fielding the next ground ball, hitting the cutoff, or coming back after the umpire just hosed him on strike two, he has a routine where he allows himself to take a deep breath, relax, and get back into playing the game one-pitch-at-a-time. He's able to battle and fight; to have a chance to take a good quality swing on a good pitch, giving us an opportunity for that ball to find some area out there where it can impact the entire game.

Our guys are really good at handling adversity. We played a 3-A school that was a good-quality, state-tournament type of team and had been there quite a few times. The coach came up to us after the game and said, "I was really impressed with your guys; I've never seen you play before but I'm really impressed with how your guys handled themselves. They just never quit." We were down 5-2 going into the fourth inning, but we battled back, scored six unanswered runs, and won 8-5. I saw that as a testament to our guys and how they go about being 1-Pitch Warriors.

ROUTINES—IMPORTANT PART OF PROGRAM

BC: Talk about the routine at the plate and on the mound of the 1-Pitch Warrior, and the importance of breathing in the routine.

JD: It's something we talk about from the first practice and throughout the season. I can pretty much tell you when a guy on our team is going to hit the ball hard. That's how well I know our guys' routines and how diligently they go about taking that deep breath. Every guy's got a different way of doing it but there's some sort of deep breath involved on a focal point. They all do it and it helps them to "slow the game down."

We practice fast so we can slow it down. We never want to let the game speed up on us; we want it to speed up on our opponent. –Whether we're in the field, on the mound, or in the batter's box, we want to play it one-pitch-at-a-time. We use our routines every pitch. The routine gets our guys locked into where they need to be, when they need to be there.

That's a key phrase for us, as well—"lock it in." Lock it in means to get that routine going and get back to your plan. One-pitch-at-a-time, be a one-pitch warrior, and let's see what happens with the results, because we can never control the results.

MENTAL IMAGERY IN PRACTICE

BC: What about mental imagery? Is that something you guys use at all? Do you as a coach use it with them to prepare, or do you ask them to use it in practice, or in games?

JD: At the beginning of the year, I thought that was one of the things we were lacking. I told them, as soon as we started with winter workouts, that I'd challenge them to go through just five minutes a day, if they could before the season started, to look at plays they need to make and how they want to swing the bat and make pitches. I wanted them to visualize going through the whole process; the routine of what they're going to do before they get in the box.

I also said, "Let's not just think about driving a ball out of the ballpark, or off the fence, or making a great diving play, but let's also visualize what you're going to do after you just threw a ball away." How you respond to adversity is more important to me than making a great play or hitting the double. Handling adversity is going to take you a long way because every one of us is going to get a bad call. Every one of us is going to have a strikeout in a game or make an error. The most important thing is how we handle it. What are we going to do to let it go and get to the next pitch?

I challenge them to go through their release and know what they are going to do after those things happen. Going through their release is important and we feel that it helps us win games.

Our offensive philosophy is BASE2, where we want to have Big Innings, we want to Answer Back, we want to Score First, we want to Extend the Lead, and we want to score with Two Outs. Defensively, we want to avoid those same things. So far, this season, our defense has been awesome. In thirty-seven games, we have given up only six unearned runs. Part of that is learning to focus on what we can control and what we need to do to be successful—our defensive routine of stepping into our circle of focus and playing it one pitch at a time.

THE STREAK

BC: Let's talk about the streak. A lot of times success will breed complacency. In a game like baseball, where the best team never wins but it's always the team that plays the best that does, how have you been able to maintain that level of performance over two years and eighty games?

JD: We have an extremely talented team. Last year, we led the state, not just in our class but in the entire state, and in almost every offensive category. Then to top it off, we also had the most shutouts, the most strikeouts, pitching-wise. We weren't a one-dimensional team and we aren't this year, either. We're second in home runs and we're still leading the state in strikeouts. So we have an enormous amount of talent and a very deep pitching staff, which at the 1-A level is pretty uncommon. If you've got one really good guy, you've got a chance, but we've got probably three or four guys who are really, really good and would be number ones in just about everyone else's program. Then, we've got other guys who could pick up innings for us on the mound.

That physical talent is part of it, but at some point you figure you're going to get beat by somebody because you have an off night or run into a good pitcher. Our guys have just stuck with the process. I'm trying to get them ready for every game the best I can and to avoid having an off night. I think it's a testament to how we go about our batting practice and what we do pre-game, because we don't really practice all that much once the season starts.

We have an hour before our game and then we get on the bus, or we have an hour before our home game, and that's our practice, really. So that's when we have to get our ground balls and our fly balls in and do all of our work in the cages to get ready. We have a lot of guys who are extremely competitive. We have a two-time state wrestling champion, who will probably win his third this year as a senior. He went undefeated as a junior, and his winner's mentality is contagious on our team. You talk about a streak; he's the one with the longest streak on our team. He hasn't lost in wrestling or in baseball for two years.

We have guys who just love to win and love to compete. They have also truly bought into the mental-game philosophy that you helped bring to the table for us, Brian, and I tried to implement in our program. I think the combination of the two has been our formula for success.

ADVICE FOR COACHES – BE DETAIL-ORIENTED

BC: If you had to offer a bit of advice to high school and college coaches around the country, something that you have done that has been successful, what would that one thing be?

JD: Be detail-oriented in everything you do. Whether it's the way we take batting practice, or how we chart our guys during the game, I try to break it down into a science and get as much information as I can during the process.

We put emphasis on quality at-bats and bunting—that's part of our process. If we do that during practice, I think we're going to do it during the game. Putting pressure on them through competition in practice translates into a more competitive team come game time.

Make practice as game-like as possible, and in the games, focus on the process, never the outcome. We're charting quality at-bats, we're charting balls and strikes for our pitchers and quality innings. When you have a system that you believe in that you can present to your team, it's going to rub off on your players.

Players are going to find success through the process. When they can stay positive and embrace adversity, good things are going to happen. It's about creating a system that will run itself, whether you are there as the coach or not. We've been pretty fortunate with the guys we have, but our system is more important than any one of us. We've got a whole other JV team that's doing the same thing, and on a nightly basis, it's the system that wins games for us, not necessarily our players.

SYSTEMS = SUCCESS

BC: Establishing a system of excellence and a right and wrong way to do things—from the way you stand for the National Anthem, to the way you take batting practice, to the way you clean up the dugout after games—and having systems for all those little things, make it so there are no little things, which makes success happen more consistently.

JD: Exactly. I think we found a system that works and we're always trying to find better ways to improve it and things to implement that we think will work better. As of now, what we're doing seems to be working pretty well. The system has got to be there, there's no doubt about that. You can't have kids who don't know what's going on out there.

1-PW POINTS FOR REVIEW:

- A 1-Pitch Warrior is a player who plays the game one-pitch-at-a-time, even in the face of adversity.

- Focusing on a focal point and taking a deep breath is a way of slowing the game down.

- Great coaches have systems within their program that are repeatable and can be implemented at any level of their program.

- "Lock it in" means getting back to your routine.

NOTES:

NOTES:

_____

_____

_____

_____

_____

_____

_____

_____

_____

_____

_____

_____

_____

_____

_____

_____

_____

_____

_____

_____

_____

_____

_____

_____

_____

_____

_____

Learning how to master the process of thinking will lead you to productive thinking. If you can develop the discipline of good thinking and turn it into a lifetime habit, then you will be successful and productive all of your life.

One day in the ground I will rest
Until that day I will give my best
With every minute I put in it
I will work hard and win it.
Because you see, it is not the result that makes the man,
It is sticking to the process and the plan.
So, even if you don't finish first,
Know it could always be worse.
Keep your mind clear,
Live in the now, live in the here.
As you give and as you live,
See the big picture and always have good perspective.
Treat each day as your last,
Live in the present and not the past.
Today is a gift, treat it well.
Remember even those at the top surely fell.
They were great and controlling their A.P.E. (Attitude, Perspective, and Effort)
One last thing to mention,
It's called the difference-maker, so pay attention.
If you want to make the most of your todays,
Having a great attitude is the last piece that pays.
So, whatever it is you want to do,
Go out, remember the Ps and make it happen for you!

Coach Justin Dehmer

The principles and philosophies that are addressed in this book will go far beyond the foul lines on a baseball field. Becoming a 1-Pitch Warrior is a life skill that players will be able to use on homework assignments that they do not want to do, but know need to be finished; a paper they need to research and write; dealing with tough, life situations that we all face throughout our lives; and in many other situations. "Coaching" is much more about teaching life lessons through sports, than learning fundamentals of how to field a groundball and hit a curveball.

Some say sports teach life lessons and players learn character through sports. I could not disagree more. Sports only reveal what players have developed personally over time; the game will not teach character, it will only reveal it. This is where I believe most players/coaches/programs lack the knowledge to actually teach character, or what some would call mental toughness. The Guide to Mental Toughness will unlock a vocabulary, and a way of doing things that are proactive in teaching a mental toughness so 1-Pitch Warrior status can be achieved, instead of just hoping players acquire it through playing and learning it on their own. I firmly believe that mental toughness is a skill that can be learned just like catching a fly ball or laying a bunt down. It is not something that is innate. Family background, life experiences, past successes and failures, and many other things will be determining factors in what is brought to the table, but this sort of toughness is a true skill. Mastering the mental game will unlock untapped potential players never knew existed.

THE FOUNDATIONS OF THE 1-PITCH WARRIOR

I needed something to motivate and inspire players so that they would know that we had a plan to defeat the best teams around. I love to come up with a slogan for every year and unveil it to the players like it is some new sports car at an auto show. I came up with the saying, "5 Ps to get to 7." The idea came from some concepts I learned from Brian Cain. It established our goal of getting to the state tournament to play for a state title. The first five Ps were:

1) PERSPECTIVE

2) PROCESS

3) POSITIVE ATTITUDE

4) PRESENT MOMENT

5) QUALITY PRACTICE OR PREPARATION

The last two Ps were "PRINCIPAL PARK," the location where the Iowa state tournament is played every year. I really believed that if we could get everyone to concentrate on the 5 Ps of Peak Performance and to adopt them as our team philosophy, that we would win more games. Not only would they help us become better, but also I thought that, in the effort to learn the 5 Ps, many of the problems we had the season before would fade away. Committing to the 5 Ps of Peak Performance were not going to automatically make us better, but I believed that they would give us an edge on the competition.

PERSPECTIVE

"When you change the way you look at things, the things you look at change."

Dr. Wayne Dyer

This was huge for me as a coach. I thought this should be our first priority: to teach players that what they do on a daily basis should be viewed through the right lens. I wanted to make sure that our players understood that baseball is just a game. When

I was playing, sometimes I behaved as if it were life or death. If I had had a better perspective on things, I think it would have made the game much easier on me, and consequently, I would have enjoyed the game and my teammates more. As coaches, we constantly remind players that this is not something they should take too seriously but it is also not something they should take for granted. They have the opportunity to play in one of very few 1-A programs in the state that has a rich tradition. At the same time, we want them to know that playing baseball is a gift to be treasured and enjoyed while it lasts. No one gets to play forever. The bottom line is to have fun and enjoy every moment.

The one thing that I now understand is that, if you want to get a point across and make sure that it is constantly in the back of your players' minds, you must advertise what you are selling. The number one selling hamburger in the world is McDonald's, for a reason. The number one soda in the world is Coke. Why? They advertise the most! McDonald's definitely doesn't make the best hamburger I have ever tasted and you can always buy the generic cola at the store but both companies do know how to advertise their products. Our product was the 5 Ps of Peak Performance. I wanted to sell my players on the fact that, if we committed to the Ps, then we would see results. To that end, I made a poster that had the word "perspective" in the middle. I picked images that were captivating and that were events that the players knew about. I picked pictures from tragedies such as Hurricane Katrina, 9/11, floods in the Midwest, and soldiers at war. These were things that they had witnessed in their lifetime and could relate to and visualize. I put all of these images on a big poster board and laminated it. I placed it in our dugout for players to see at every practice and every game. It was a reminder for them, an advertisement for them, that when things were going bad, they could always be worse. They get to play a game that they love, spend time with friends, and make memories that will last forever. They could be on a battlefield, or their house could be destroyed in a flood. It is much tougher to get really angry about your performance, or lack thereof, when you come back into the dugout and see this huge "perspective" poster staring at you. I have had very few problems with anger management issues, not because there are consequences if a player throws a bat or helmet, but because we take the time to talk about a proper perspective with our players. It gets them in a positive state of mind for when things go wrong. It is baseball and things never go the way you think they will. With perspective, we are always making sure that players understand the first rule about being mentally tough: you have very little control of what goes on around you, but total control of how you respond to it. The second rule is that you must be in control of yourself, before you can control your performance. We stress that thoughts lead to actions, and actions produce results. If my players have a good perspective going in, I thought we would be on the right foot and we could then begin to work on the game.

Challenge: Make your own "perspective" poster. Do it as a team or just for yourself. Include meaningful events, people, places, or things that give you a positive perspective and that will help you realize that today is a great opportunity to play baseball, to go to school, to go to work, etc. For examples of some that we have used, email me at coachd@1pitchwarrior.com.

Once you have created your poster, put it somewhere where you will see it every day. Place it in your locker, your bedroom, on your ceiling, or bathroom mirror. Advertise, advertise, and advertise! Constantly remind yourself to put things into a proper perspective and you will be surprised at the difficulties you can endure.

PROCESS

"Focus on the journey, not the destination. Joy is found not in finishing an activity but in doing it."

Greg Anderson

We try to get players to believe in the process to bring about the results we want. Baseball is a brutal game, riddled with failure. You can deliver a perfect pitch and it can still be hit out of the park. On the offensive side of things, you can hit the ball harder than you ever have in your life and someone can make a great play so you have nothing to show for it. That is how most people would look at it. We strive to teach our players that there are things that we can control and things we cannot. You cannot control the other team from making an amazing play in the hole at shortstop, throwing you out at first after the first baseman picks it in the dirt. All you can control is whether you take a good swing at a good pitch. If you do, then you can be satisfied with your at-bat. We want players to hold their heads high even when things go wrong because they took care of things on their end. Our process is to become focused on the things that we can control and not get wrapped up in the things we cannot control.

Remember that the number one rule of mental toughness is that you have very little control of what goes on around you, but you are in total control of how you respond to it. We want our players to come away from getting robbed by a great play with the feeling that they did all they could. Are they going to be discouraged? Sure, but we want that to be a short-lived feeling followed quickly by understanding that they did all they could. At times, I have seen other players and even some of our own turn that type of at-bat into a slump. They begin pressing and trying to do too much when they were already doing enough. Baseball is an unfair game and players and coaches must be able to deal with frustration on a regular basis. If batters keep taking a good approach at the plate, then success is bound to find them eventually. Our process-based philosophy is governed by the K.I.S.S. principle: Keep It Simple Stupid (or Keep It Super Simple). The only thing our hitters are trying to do is hit the ball hard. Beyond that, it is out of their control. We do not want players worried about outcome-oriented goals, such as how many hits they have, or how many RBIs, doubles, or homeruns they are accumulating. If they are concentrating on the process of hitting the ball hard, the stats will be there at the end of the season. Winning is a by-product of doing many little things correctly throughout the game. If we can stay with our process-based philosophy, we will have a great chance to achieve a quality outcome in the end.

By focusing on the things you can control rather than outcomes, you allow yourself to become more successful, almost instantly. If we look at a 10 at-bat section of a season and you get three hits in those 10 ABs, some players will look at that as .300. Let's then say you hit three other balls hard, but got out on the remaining 6 ABs. You did what you could control and did your job. Now, that hitter can view himself as a .600 hitter, twice the hitter he was before just by being process-oriented rather than outcome-oriented. In later chapters, I will go in-depth as to how we measure these behaviors and the criteria we use to calculate what a hitter can control. It is in the perspective you give your players and the process they use that will determine how they view their performance and that will improve play and attitude.

"It is good to have an end to journey towards; but it is the journey that matters in the end."

Ursula Le Guin

The same thing happens on the pitching side of things. Ask yourself this question: What is the pitcher's job? Answers always vary from "to get outs" to "win the game." This is one of the biggest pet peeves I have in the way baseball is measured and calculated. A pitcher is credited with a W or L every night. But, he can pitch great and lose, or pitch terribly and win. It makes no sense and is often an unfair way to assess a pitcher. It goes back to measuring our player's performance based on what he can control on the field and staying away from outcome goals, like winning the game or hitting .300. I have asked coaches and players all over the country about what the pitcher's job is, and I always hear different things. But, the only thing we can control on the mound is whether we throw a strike or not, and even then, it is really out of our control because we all know umpires are not perfect. We tell our pitchers that there is no such thing as a strike zone; there is only an umpire zone. It changes every night and we must adjust accordingly. We are asking our pitchers to throw it around the zone. If we throw strikes on a consistent basis, then the strikeouts and wins will come, but a pitcher is not in control of whether he wins or loses a game. It is a tough concept for some pitchers to grasp. We ask our pitchers to be focused only on what they can control—throwing good pitches one pitch at a time. Hence, the 1-Pitch Warrior Style!

Our players have done a tremendous job at being what we call a "1-Pitch Warrior"—locking it in on every pitch, trying to do all they can, staying with the process, and controlling what they can control. It prevents us from not getting too high and not getting too low, because there is always a next pitch to hit or throw. I am extremely confident that focusing on the process instead of the outcome has been the key to winning 88 games in a row along with three straight state championships.

Two things we talk about when trying to implement the process of focusing on what you can control is to control your A.P.E. and the "next 200 feet" concept.

A.P.E. stands for the three things that you can control in this world—Attitude, Perspective, and Effort. We want players to understand that by learning to control these three things they can learn to focus their attention on being process-based players. If a player has a terrible attitude about his previous at-bat, it will affect how his ability to do his job on the next at-bat, or pitch, or fielding opportunity. Getting players—or in my case, students in my classroom—to buy into the A.P.E. philosophy, works wonders and gets kids to be responsible for their actions, or lack thereof. The process can only work if all three things are present. It is hard to be present without doing all of them. Going back to the idea of advertising what you want to your players, one coach went so far as to have a stuffed ape in the locker room to remind his players to control their A.P.E. The stuffed ape was much like the perspective poster I put up in our dugout.

THE NEXT 200 FEET CONCEPT

If you are standing in Los Angeles with just a flashlight and your family is in New York and there was total darkness throughout the entire country, could you get there only using the flashlight? No daylight, no other lights working other than your flashlight? The answer to this question is YES.

How would you accomplish such a feat? You would start the journey walking, knowing that there is a way to get there. One part is having faith that the road will lead you where you want to go, but the other part is worrying only about the process and not the outcome. Even with only the 200 feet you can see in front of you with your flashlight, you will eventually get to New

York. Invest only in the next 200 feet. This is what it means to be a 1-Pitch Warrior: all efforts are about the next pitch. In the classroom, worry only about the next problem. At work, worry only about the next client. Walk the next 200 feet, then the next 200, and then the next. PROCESS! Work it and let the results take care of themselves. Plan the work and then work the plan.

Turning this process-based strategy into a daily routine is the ultimate goal. The tools that we give to players for on-the-field use are not merely to help them be better baseball players or to win games; they are strategies to help them tackle everything that life will throw at them. They will all go through tough times. Some may face the loss of a loved one, unemployment, and other tragedies in the future. If they can use the 5 Ps to get through those tough times, then my job as a coach has been more than I could ever expect it to be. Playing a sport does not just teach about winning and losing; it teaches players about life and how to work through all the twists and turns that will undoubtedly come their way.

"A journey of a thousand miles must begin with a single step."

Lao-Tsu

I have not only tried to teach my players to understand and use the 5 Ps of Peak Performance, but I have also tried to be a role model to them by using them in my own daily life. My wife was training for her first-ever half-marathon one summer. We were at her parents' house for the 4th of July weekend and she was talking about how she was going to train the next morning at the high school on the all-weather track. She said she was going to run 8 miles and her family was amazed. Then, I opened my big mouth and told everyone that I could do it, too. I am in shape and like to work out, but rarely run. That summer, I had not run more than one mile combined, let alone 8 miles at one time. I knew going into it that it would be mind-over-matter, because physically I had not trained for anything even close to those 8 miles. Will over Skill.

The first few miles were not too bad. I hung in there and stayed at a good pace. No pain and no problems. Once the fourth mile came, I was starting to hurt. With the dreaded side cramp, it was getting harder and harder for me to get some good air and I was running poorly. The pain in my side hindered my strides. The muscles in my legs and calves started getting tight, as well. But, I was still determined to get to the finish. I was not going to stop and not going to quit. When adversity came our way on the field, we had a plan—our 5 Ps plan. Now, I found myself in a situation where I needed to be focused on the process instead of the outcome. I knew I wanted to get to the end of the run, but I also knew the only way I would get to the end was if I was able to run the next 20 yards, then the next 20 yards, and continue to repeat each 20 yards until I finished. THE NEXT 20 YARDS! It worked. I started finding marks on the track ahead of me that were about 20 yards, and I would focus all of my attention and energy on getting to that mark. Once I made it to that mark, then I would find my next mark and continue the pattern. I do not know if it was because my attention was not on the pain in my side but shifted instead to the principle of the next 20 yards, but the side cramp eventually went away and I was ultimately able to finish the run without ever stopping. The next few days my body was in some serious pain and my muscles were extremely tight and sore, but I finished the "race." The feeling I had was one of accomplishment and, knowing it was because I employed the mental training that we use with our baseball team, made it even more rewarding for me. That afternoon, I told the team of my adventure and explained to them how I did it. It was a great teachable moment for my players and related so well to exactly what we believe in.

We won 88 games in a row—at one point a national record! It was unreal! Even though I lived it and watched every pitch, it is still hard for me to actually believe. Winning 88 games in anything many would say is impossible. We were never trying to win 88 in a row. We did not set a team goal to try to win 88 in a row. That would be crazy. Once the record was within sight, however, we did want to break it, but it always was about being 1-Pitch Warriors—playing the next pitch, worrying only about what we could control, and trying to get better every day, striving for excellence.

On nearly every special occasion, I send players a text wishing them a happy birthday or a happy holiday. The Thanksgiving after our second state title, I sent a message to former and current players telling them to have a great day with their families and to dominate the turkey. Within five minutes, I received text messages back, wishing me to do the same. More than one player sent me a message saying something to the effect of "1-Scoop Warriors," "1-Bite Warriors," or "1-Bite-at-a-Time." It was a cool little moment for me to know that they believe, carry, and apply these philosophies into their everyday life…even to joke about them!

POSITIVE ATTITUDE

"Excellence is not a skill. It is an attitude."

Ralph Marston

Before you can be in control of your physical play, you must be in control of your thoughts or your attitude. Attitude is one part of your A.P.E. You can control your attitude…and only yours. It is not up to your coach, teacher, parents, pastor, or

God. It is up to you. Regardless of circumstances, having a great attitude is something we want our players to have each day they show up to the field. Whether you are in the line-up or not, or you had the best game of your life the day before, or you went 0 for 4, we don't care. What matters, is today and the attitude you bring to it. Again, thoughts become actions and actions produce results. I have a hard time recalling any players I have coached who showed up with a bad attitude and went on to have a great game. I can, however, give countless examples of players who had great attitudes and ended up having great games, unexpectedly. Our team set the national record for high school baseball with 87 wins in a row. Some people point to the fact that we had talent—which I will never deny. We absolutely were loaded with talent and even had great players on the bench who would have started on most of the teams we played. But, if talent alone won games, then why, time and time again, do we see upsets in all sports? As we progressed in the post-season, the physical talent margin of our team and the opposing team grew tighter and tighter. When the talent level is almost equal, what will make the difference? Physical talent means very little when it comes time for the final score. The 5 Ps mean much more. What is going on in players' minds plays a much bigger role in how they will perform and ultimately leads to wins and losses. It is a matter of playing better than your competition in big games. When you are riding a winning streak and are ranked #1 for two years straight, there is a huge target on your back and every game becomes a big game. Everyone wants to take down the top team and say they were the one that beat Martensdale-St. Mary's, stopping the streak. Down the line, we never beat ourselves. Our work with the mental game allowed us to do this. If you want to beat us, you will have to play better than us. Remember what I said about thoughts leading to actions. If that is true, then beating us requires the other team to be better mentally plus have the physical talent permitting both thoughts and mental toughness play out on the field. I have a hard time believing that any team out there has spent as much as, or more time talking about the only side of baseball that really matters. Most coaches are going to stress the Xs and Os of the game and there is nothing wrong with that. However, we want to be extraordinary, and to be extraordinary means you must do what the average person is not willing to do. Our players have been great about adopting the 5 Ps of being a 1-Pitch Warrior. If your attitude is not better, or at least as good, as the other team's, how can you expect to win? Attitude alone does not mean that success is going to come your way, but it gives you a much better chance that good things will occur. If you think you cannot do something, you are right. If you think you can, you just might.

Thoughts are like magnets attracting things to it. If you continue to have negative thoughts about how terrible you are at third base and why you cannot catch a ground ball, then you will continue to get more of the same negative thoughts. If you change the way you think, then the outcome will begin to change, as well. If you think you can catch a ground ball and are a good infielder, then you will be. It is not a hard concept to follow, but it is hard to put into action, because baseball is so tough on the player. It is simple: like attracts like. Think about not swinging at the curveball in the dirt and guess what you just did? Struck out by swinging at a curveball in the dirt. We tell our players to think about what they want to do; not what they want to avoid. If you have two strikes, then think about hitting a ball that is in the zone. Do not tell yourself to not swing at the ball in dirt. That is a sure way of leading back to the dugout.

Players must become highly aware of their thoughts. This is key. If they cannot control their mental state, how can we ever expect them to play well, or consistently? We teach our players a technique in which they can consciously check in, pitch-by-pitch, to ensure that they are staying focused on the task at hand and maintaining a positive attitude. I will discuss more about this when we talk about the Present Moment.

We are all in control of our attitudes and possess the power to change them good or bad, at any moment. Even if our players are tired, or have had a bad day, we ask them to change their attitude once they are at practice or at the game, because we know that "like attracts like" and, if they continue with their current attitude, things are not going to go well for them or the team. We ask them to "fake it 'til you make it."

You do not have to be an all-state player to act like one. You do not have to be a .300 hitter before you act like one. I tell them to "act, as if." Act, as if, you are the starting centerfielder; act, as if, you are the district champions; act, as if, you are the state champions. If you act this way, then you will do what these people do, giving yourself the best possible chance of becoming that kind of player.

When I first started coaching, I knew a little about the game, but not nearly as much as I do now. Although I was a young coach, it did not stop me from acting as if I knew what I was doing, nor did it stop me from behaving as a great coach would. Even though I did not have state championships under my belt, I still thought of myself as that type of coach. Consequently, I did the things that state championship coaches do. In time, the thoughts that I had been having for so many years came true. Like attracts like. Thoughts become actions.

"If we all did the things we are capable of doing, we would literally astound ourselves."

Thomas Edison

One thing I do when I show up to the field, no matter what, is "fake it 'til I make it." If I have had a long day, I don't let my players know it. If my kids were terrible or something happened with the school administration, or my wife, or my family, I never bring it to the field. I leave it in my car, literally. When I get back in my car to go home, it is my choice to pick it back up or not. I try to hold myself to the same accountability that I ask of my players. When I show up, I ask the players I come in contact with how they are doing. The first time I do this with a player, he usually gives me the typical teenage answer of "fine" or "okay." Then, I ask them again. They may indeed be just fine or okay, but I ask them again until I get the answer I want to hear, which is a positive one. An answer like "great" or "amazing" means I stop asking you how you are doing. They are "faking it 'til they make it." It is hard to say you are doing "amazing" without actually feeling that way on the inside. If we feel great or amazing then we can have good positive thoughts. If we have good positive thoughts, then we can accomplish more great or amazing things, which in turn, leads to quality play during the game, or being a great teammate, etc. I want the players to feel amazing and they might just play amazingly. I have taken a lot of time to make our uniforms look good. We have three different tops that we can wear, plus our undershirt if it is an extremely hot day. Our players really like the look of our uniforms. I did this on purpose; not because I am into fashion, but because I want them to look good. A few of our players would say, "look good, feel good, play good." I believe it and so do they. It all plays a part; there are no small things.

PRESENT MOMENT

"Do not dwell in the past, do not dream of the future, concentrate the mind on the present moment."

Buddha

After all the work we do with the other Ps (Perspective, Process, and Positive Attitude), this one may be the most important and it has great implications beyond baseball. This is the analogy I use for "Present Moment" when it comes to coaching: If I have a player with the most amazing swing, but he cannot focus his attention in the game, whether it is a big game or against a team we should definitely beat, how valuable is that beautiful swing of his? On the other hand, I may have a player with a swing that could use some work, but he can concentrate in pressure situations and focus on the present moment and the current task. He is a player who keeps things simple in his head and does not let outside factors like the crowd, the base runners, the coaches, the other team, the umpire, or the weather get in the way of doing the job. Who are you going to have in the line-up?

I know the player I want in the line-up. To me, it is a no-brainer. We all have seen Michael Jordan get in "the zone." I would say that he was the best at staying in the present moment. The "zone" is nothing other than an intense focus that allows skill to shine in pressure situations. Some say he blocks out the crowd. I would say that his thought process helps the crowd fade away through his 1-Shot Warrior Mentality. Michael Jordan is an amazing player and one of the best, if not the best. He was an astoundingly talented player, but what was overlooked many times, was his mental approach and how he was able to defy the odds, time and time again, with winning shots. I really think that mental preparation is a teachable, coachable skill, and not something innate. I think anyone can learn it and apply the same concepts that helped Jordan hit that buzzer beater from the foul line against the Cavs. To this day, I can still picture that shot in my mind. Being a "1-Pitch Warrior," a "1-Shot Warrior," or a "1-Possession Warrior," is something that we all can become. I think it is also important to note that Jordan, although being remembered for making so many game-winning shots and playing big when it mattered most, also failed 26 times to win a game. Failure is never final. Flush it. Press on.

THE Rs

Within planning for the present moment, there are five key strategies that players need to master to create the consistent focus that will lead to consistent play and results:

1) ROUTINES

2) REHEARSE

3) RECOGNIZE

4) RELEASE

5) REFOCUS

This is a cyclical process that starts again after a pitch or play is over.

This is how we do things. We do not tell our players that this guarantees success; we just tell them that, if we can work the process, it will likely improve our chances down the road. We want them to commit to the idea of being a 1-Pitch Warrior. If you ask your team what is the most important part of the game, they will have a variety of answers. We want our players to fully understand that nothing is more important than what is about to happen right now. They can only control the present, their focus, and the mindset that they bring to it. They cannot change the past. Errors, bad calls, and missed opportunities must be forgotten and not carried on to the next pitch. They change the present by fully embracing it with their ability to lock in and compete in the task. By doing this, they give themselves the best chance to improve in the future. One of my favorite sayings is something I have shared with the players on our team on more than one occasion:

"The past is history,

The future is a mystery,

They call it the present because it is a gift."

For players to be in the present moment, they must master the repetition in the cycle of Rs.

ROUTINES

We have to understand that focusing attention for many short intervals during a game is the key to baseball. We cannot expect players to be watching and focusing on the game continuously. That is impossible and no one can do that. We just need them to go in and out of focus many, many times during a game, as demonstrated in the Kevin Costner movie, *For the Love of the Game*. In the film, the pitcher uses a routine called "clear the mechanism," and all becomes centered around his present moment. The crowd fades, he doesn't see the fans, or the other team—it is just the catcher and the pitcher on the mound. The character has a routine that he uses which Hollywood glamorizes, but it is something to this effect that we want our players to develop for their own routines.

There are many different routines out there that, as a young kid, growing up watching baseball, you try to emulate, but the one that is right for you is the one that makes you comfortable. We tell our players that they can do anything they want, as long as it has these three things in it:

1) A point of reference

2) A deep breath

3) Positive self-talk

One technique that we have given players is to start with both hands on the bat, one foot in the box, and to focus on the trademark or logo on their bat. This centers their attention; it is a checkpoint for them to understand where their current thoughts are taking them. It allows them to do a self-check and to evaluate their self-talk. If their focus or self-talk is not there, then they step out of the box until it is. After they have decided that they are ready for the pitch, they will take a deep breath—we call this getting big. We want them to fill up their lungs with as much air as possible, and then slowly blow it out. As they blow out the air, they are having thoughts about what it is that they need to do during the pitch. This routine gets them focused on the hitting side of baseball, saying something to the effect of "see ball, hit ball," "swing at a strike," "see the ball big," or "good swing at a good pitch."

An example of a pitching routine might be to have the pitcher address the rubber with his head down, feet on the rubber, and then focus his attention on something on the ground. It can be his shoelaces, a rock, or the logo on top of his shoes. It just needs to be a focal point of some kind. Then, like a batter, they are going to get a big, deep breath, and blow it out. As they relax, their positive self-talk must take over—something like "pound the zone" or "hit the glove."

Fielding may be the toughest place to have focus, because the act is so unexpected. Players have no idea when they may be involved in a play directly and could go an entire game without ever getting a play. We try to have a process for this and we flat-out tell the players that they do not need to focus all the time when they are on defense, but to imagine that there is a circle where they are playing and every time they are in the circle, it is time to go through their defensive routine. After the pitch is over and the ball is secure, then they can walk around, look around, etc. It would be unreasonable for us to ask for total and continuous attention of our players for the two to two and half hours we will be playing. We just need them to use their routine of going in and out of focus. Once they get back into their circle of focus, then they are to do a routine like the others I have talked about. This would include a deep breath, followed by exhaling and saying something like "react to the ball," "go get it," or "see it off the bat." The routine in the field is critical to avoid one of the pitfalls of baseball—boredom. You may go a few games without ever having to make a play, but you must always be prepared to make one on every pitch.

Have your players come up with their own lingo and self-talk. It is best if it comes from them rather than you spoon-feeding them how to do it. They will have a sense of ownership if they come up with it themselves but give them some examples to help them. Nobody likes it when they feel forced to do something. Provide suggestions for your team but let them decide how their routine will play out. The self-talk should be a one liner and be task-oriented, not outcome-oriented. Sayings like "get a hit" are ones we want to stay away from, because we know that getting a hit is out of our control. Hitting the ball hard is something we can control. If you are looking for a good list to help generate ideas for self-talk check out www.1pitchwarrior.com and the 1-Pitch Warrior Program that includes the implementation of all the key concepts and features of this book.

We go so far as to make players write down what their routines are going to look like. We make them write down one for each part of the game—hitting, defense, base running, and if they are a pitcher, pitching. Again, the write-up must include the three things we feel are necessary for a good routine. I read them and if I am satisfied with what the players wrote down on paper, then they have their routine for the year. If it is not good enough, I give them some suggestions and have them go back and fix it.

REHEARSE

"Excellence is an art won by training and habituation. We do not act rightly because we have virtue or excellence, but we rather have those because we have acted rightly. We are what we repeatedly do. Excellence, then, is not an act, but a habit."

Aristotle

The next R is to rehearse it. Just like any skill, we must practice it. The mental game is no different. Actors have a script that they read and reread before their big moment on camera. If they do not get it right, they have a chance for another take. Sports are not so kind; you get one take and if you do not get it right, you must live with the consequences. It makes sense to have our players have a script for their performance, as well. If they write it down, they become the writer, director, and the actor of the motion picture called "Our Season." We do not have players map out the game and the plays they will make, because much of what happens in the course of a game is out of our control. The one thing that players are in control of is their pre-pitch routine on defense, when pitching, or when hitting. Once it is down on paper, it becomes their script for the game during every pitch.

Throughout the course of practice, players have many opportunities to rehearse their routines. You can have players use their routines at the beginning of drills in the cage, during BP, during live scrimmages, or during hitting situations that you might do during the course of practice. Each must know his routine, because when the game is on the line is not the ideal time to start using a routine. We want the consistent practice of it to produce consistent results. A routine is not something to keep in your back pocket for when you need it; you need to use it all the time.

We try to come up with pressure situations each day in practice so that our players compete against each other in situational games, or even for Gatorades. Something is going to be on the line when we practice and this helps practice feel important and game-like. We try to make everything game-like, or even more intense than a game. Without making practice tough and game-like, you do not give your players the chance to practice the mental game and become 1-Pitch Warriors. Allowing players to know what pressure is going to feel like, means they can practice responding with their routines. Remember—the only thing players can control is their Attitude, Perspective, and Effort. Having a routine that players can go to when things get tough is essential to keeping their A.P.E. in check.

We, as coaches, must be there to coach them when to lock in on those routines. If I see a kid is thinking about the bad pitch that he just swung at, I tell him to step out, go through his routine, and "flush it." The routine lets them slow the game down and get back to playing one-pitch-at-a-time. It is a trigger that tells them they need to be better focused, that they need to get back to "see ball, hit ball," or "to see the catcher's target and throw it there." Task-oriented, not outcome-oriented, is what we want. We want our players to experience these situations during practice; it makes them more comfortable with the uncomfortable. We essentially create pressure during practice, so that players have the chance to fail. We want them to face adversity on a daily basis and to respond to it so it is not a performance crusher. When it happens in a game, our players know that they have been in this situation before and they know how to handle it. If they feel comfortable, this leads to confidence; if they feel confident, then they have a great chance of performing well. But, first they have to know they can master a situation before it can ever happen.

We have some terminology that goes along with letting players know that we want them to go through their routines in practice or games. One is to "Get B.I.G." This reminds them that they need to take that big, deep breath that is part of every player's routine—get big. We want them to fill their lungs with as much air as possible, and then slowly blow all the air out through their mouth. Although, compared to other sports, baseball is considered a slow game, to a player it can feel like things are moving at a million miles an hour. Having the comfort of their routines can significantly change the pace of the game.

We have all been in a situation where we have twenty things going on at once and it feels overwhelming. Life is moving at light speed. That is actually what the game of baseball can feel like, and before you know it, your at-bat is over and you just struck out. I consider this a waste of an at-bat, because the player who lets the situation control him is not in control of himself. The game got the best of him and he let it happen. A great routine, without the rehearsal element, will result in players who cannot handle adversity and the big moment. They become enmeshed in the uncontrollable instead of focusing on what they can control.

RECOGNIZE

"I think self-awareness is probably the most important thing to becoming a champion."

Billie Jean King

We give our players a color spectrum to identify where their thoughts are during the course of the game. The spectrum goes from green to yellow to red. We want them to be able to be aware of which part of the spectrum they are experiencing. Green is all systems are go, yellow means that they are in a spot where things can get worse in a hurry if they do not take care of it right away, and red means things are out of control. When players are playing their best, they are usually in green, not worrying or dwelling on thoughts of past performances, or a bad call, or the fans, etc. We talk about understanding the situations in a game when things can take a turn for the worse. These situations could be a bad swing at a bad pitch, not swinging at a good pitch, errors, wild-pitches, pass balls, missing a sign, not getting a bunt down, giving up a hit, a bad call, walking a hitter, hitting a batter, and more. Again, recognizing is all about knowing the game and being aware of a player's emotional state at all times during the game; and knowing the situations that will lead him to encountering yellow lights and red lights that could affect performance in a negative way. During the course of the game, we are trying to play in the green at all times and win as many pitches as we possibly can. Remember, being task-oriented—winning this pitch—is something that a player can have within his sights. Winning the game is not. If we win more pitches than the other team throughout the course of the game, we are giving our team a great opportunity to win in the end. This is why it is so important not to give away at-bats or pitches on the mound.

RELEASE

"Stress is not what happens to us. It's our response TO what happens. And RESPONSE is something we can choose."

Maureen Killoran

When first implementing the mental strategies needed to be more consistent, we really need players to understand what it feels like, and conversely, what having negative thoughts does to them. Most players do not really understand how these thoughts affect their performances. To demonstrate, we use an analogy that a bad thought, a bad game, etc., is like a brick. We will then hand an actual brick to a player and ask him if he can hold the brick and put it in his back pocket for five minutes. The answer is always yes. We take it a step further and ask him if he can hold it for 15 minutes; again, the answer is yes. We start throwing out longer times, such as half an hour—about the time it will take players to get another at-bat during the course of a game. Players really start to see the weight of what they are holding or have in their back pockets. Finally, I ask them to go home with the brick and carry it around all the next day until they come back to the field for our next game.

It is like a light bulb goes off in players' heads. At this point, they start to understand the power of their thoughts. They see that they may have let their past performance predict their future performance, because of that mental brick they were carrying around. The analogy works. The exercise helps players make sense of it all. The negative thoughts—the yellow and red lights—that they have during the course of the game are the mental bricks which they have the option of carrying around or not carrying around. I reiterate: players need to understand that they are in full control of how they respond. To carry, or not carry the mental brick is a crucial question within baseball games. I believe it is during these moments in the course of a contest that the game is either won or lost. Over the course of our streak and championships, I remember winning the closest games, not always because we played great, but because the other teams had moments in which they could not overcome the mental bricks that are a part of the game. We were able to capitalize on their inabilities to move past a bad call, walking a batter, an error, etc.

As you can see, we use many physical items to unlock the mental game. We want players to do something physical to help them with the things that are going on inside their heads. A brick, posters, and routines can actually help with implementing and understanding how to become a 1-Pitch Warrior.

Once players appreciate the weight of their thoughts and realize that, no matter where they go, if they keep thinking about the bad play they made, there is no way that they can perform at their best. They must deal with the previous play. I would not want to try to field another ground ball with a mental brick in my back pocket. Ask your players if they think they can play their best, when it matters most, with the "mental brick" in their back pocket.

We want to create an attitude that, no matter what happens, players will move on to the next pitch. We have many sayings for this but the one we use the most for this is to "flush it." It is another visual for players to think about. They throw the negative moments and the thoughts that go along with them into a toilet and "flush it" so that they can get back to playing the game as a 1-Pitch Warrior. They are getting rid of the crap, the mental crap!

"Losers live in the past. Winners learn from the past and enjoy working in the present toward the future."

Denis Waitley

This is where the routine the players have created is so important and the rehearsal will be so effective. Moments of bad play and bad calls are inevitable during the course of play and are always magnified by real-game situations. We tell our players to trust in their routines and use them when the yellow and red lights pop up, because they will! It is how we handle these situations that determines the game and our season. Their routines will allow them to "flush it" and get refocused on what really matters— the next pitch. Some of the other sayings that we use in these situations are "So what, next pitch," "Get B.I.G.," and "So long, move on."

To promote this way of thinking, we have a brick that we keep in our dugout and even take with us when we play away games. Written on the brick, is "Flush It" to remind players what we are about. These strategies are designed to help players handle the adversity that is a part of any sport. Baseball, in particular, comes with a great amount of adversity built into the game. I believe that sports are a teacher of life skills and I know that there is no better tool for players, or anyone, to possess than that of overcoming adversity. Drugs, depression, and all the other serious issues our society is suffering stem from people being unable to "Flush It." There is something that they cannot get past and, instead of playing one-pitch-at-a-time, they turn to other ways to try to play the next pitch. Unfortunately, it never works. I hope that in some way we are not only helping players to be their best on the field but to be even better at the game of life, which has a fair amount of adversity, as well.

REFOCUS

"Our thoughts create our reality – where we put our focus is the direction we tend to go."

Peter McWilliams

The last R to complete the cycle is to refocus. Once players have a routine in place and are given the opportunities to rehearse it repeatedly in a structured setting with a coach who knows what he is looking for, players will have the ability to recognize situations in the course of a practice or game and can respond accordingly. They will use all of what we have talked about to begin the refocusing process for themselves. The last step is continuing the process as many times as necessary during the course of a game.

Focus is crucial to help players play their best. To play big, players need to "get B.I.G.," follow their routines, trust in them, and stay process-oriented, letting the results take care of themselves. We want to give our players the best opportunity to play well and to focus on more pitches during the game than the other team. This gives us a distinct advantage, without even considering talent, or who is pitching, or taking any of the other variables into consideration. Refocusing, no matter if the previous play or pitch was a good or bad outcome, is the cornerstone of our mental approach and has allowed us to battle back from some late-game deficits.

During our third state title run in the semi-final, we were down to our last strike on two different occasions yet rallied to score two runs to tie it. Being a 1-Pitch Warrior doesn't guarantee success, but it will give you the best chance for things to go your way. We are living, breathing proof of this and rallied in many other games throughout the 2010, 2011, 2012 seasons with the 1-Pitch Warrior Mentality.

We achieved a remarkable streak/championships, which required much more than just talented players, or even a strong will to win. No doubt these are things that contributed to what we accomplished, but I am convinced, without a shadow of a doubt, that our ability to be so consistent was because of the time and effort we placed on becoming 1-Pitch Warriors.

QUALITY PRACTICE/PREPARATION

"By failing to prepare, you are preparing to fail."

Ben Franklin

The last key element for the 5 Ps is to prepare your players by practicing in a way that matters and means something. We want our players to have the idea that we are trying to achieve excellence in execution. We want them to know that everything they do matters. Our players should feel that today is their big day; that today is all that matters; that they should make today the best day it can be. What one does when no one is watching is what matters most. Excellence is not an event—it is a lifestyle and a way of doing things that has no finish line. Champions make the most of every drill, ground ball, or fly ball. They do not just go through the motions. We tell players to go home if they are just going through the motions.

"Don't count the days, make the days count."

Muhammad Ali

Each player has an hourglass that is continually running out. There is only a finite amount of time that a player can play the game. With dedication, each may be able to extend the life of his career, but ultimately it will come to an end. We want our players to realize this for two reasons: 1) so they will work as hard as possible to become better; and 2) so that they will learn to enjoy what they have at the time and have fun.

We want players to do everything with a purpose—a purpose to get better, a purpose to beat our conference rival, a purpose to get to the state tournament, etc. To get them to focus on having a plan for improvement, we even started having players write down their Small Daily Goals for the practice before it starts. This helps make practice be much more productive. Also, it allows me to read the things that players think they need to improve. Our ideas do not always match, but it is good for me to hear it from them. While the players are stretching, I usually read their lists to give me some ideas, through his eyes, how I can help a player.

I expect only these things: Attitude, Perspective, and Effort (A.P.E.) If those are not there, then we have a discussion about making these things happen. Usually this "talk" is enough for players to make the proper changes, ensuring that the rest of practice is a productive one and we are preparing the best we can.

In 2011, about an hour or so into a practice, I was so unhappy with our lack of focus and the way that we were practicing, that I gave all the players five minutes to get their stuff and go home. Rather than suffer through a practice that was terrible and not getting any better, I sent them home. Again, it goes to what we stand for: if we are not getting any better, then why be here?

When you have a group of individuals who are all operating under the premise that working with quality in mind, we will get a little better today because of it. Imagine then how much better we will be at the end of the season, if each day we improve, even if only a little bit. If there was an easy way, then all teams would be great. If there was a short cut, we would all take it. The fact is, there are no shortcuts to being great; we all will fall short of reaching our full potential. The challenge is to see how close we can come.

I come up with practice plans that mean something. Every drill we do or every situation we run matters. It matters, because running may be on the line, or there is a competition between players, or teams within our team. We are creating pressure and adversity rather than just going through the motions. I hated most of my baseball practices in high school because it always seemed they could have been so much more productive. One player hitting batting practice, a few in the cages, and the rest standing around in the outfield is not my idea of a game-like practice. I would say most of what we do in practice is game-like or tougher. We want our players to feel the pressure and be comfortable with the uncomfortable. All other teams that do not have practices that are game-like are doing us a favor, because our team will be well-prepared for them. We take pride in knowing that we will be more prepared than every team we play. That breeds confidence!

For more on practice organization, drills, game-like practices, and the 7-disc 1-Pitch Warrior Program that will help your players and coaches become even better at the mental game, go to www.1PitchWarrior.com to order online. Other mental game products are available on the website, as well. I have to give one more shout-out to Brian Cain for his great influence on our program and the way he changed my perspective on how to coach. He has been a huge asset to our program and a great mentor for me, as he was the one who convinced me to write these 1-Pitch Warrior Books.

1-PW POINTS FOR REVIEW:

- **Understand the 5 Ps of being a 1-Pitch Warrior:**

  1) **Perspective**

  2) **Process**

  3) **Positive Attitude**

  4) **Present Moment**

  5) **Quality Practice/Preparation**

- **Have every player develop a routine that includes a deep breath, a focal point, and a process-based thought.**

- **Implement the 1-PW Cycle of Rs:**

  1) **Routines**

  2) **Rehearse**

  3) **Recognize**

  4) **Release**

  5) **Refocus**

NOTES:

www.1pitchwarrior.com

NOTES:

_____
_____
_____
_____
_____
_____
_____
_____
_____
_____
_____
_____
_____
_____
_____
_____
_____
_____
_____
_____
_____
_____
_____
_____
_____
_____
_____
_____

CHAPTER 3: HOW TO MEASURE WHAT YOU CAN CONTROL
MEASUREMENT EQUALS MOTIVATION

One thing I have tried to do is be more objective in evaluating my team. Off the field, I am a math teacher and that has certainly played a part in the number crunching that I like to do. Instead of sitting in the outfield and giving them my opinion about the game, I hoped to give my players a number and tell them this was what their performance was today. In this section, I will explain the ways we evaluate players' performances, which will also will help players in the implementation of the 5 Ps. We have tried to make everything tie in together as a seamless process so that what we measure is focused on the player's process-based (task) outcomes, and not on outcome-oriented (end result) ones. I am a firm believer that you must be able to describe what you do as a process. The next part of this book will detail the process we use both offensively and defensively.

OFFENSIVE PHILOSOPHIES

One major flaw in baseball is the way we measure and evaluate a player's performance. Most players will evaluate how well their season is going based on what their average is. In our program, we do not talk about averages and I tell my players straight-out that the only reason I keep stats is because Iowa High School Athletic Association tells me that I must. Obviously, the Association uses stats in getting players recognition like All-Conference, All-District, and All-State.

Why measure yourself on something that you cannot control? It is totally unfair in an already very difficult game. If you hit a ball hard three times during a game and get out all three times, your batting average is zero for the night and your overall for the season will go down. Players start pressing, thinking that they need to do better, when in reality, they did their job!

We have found better ways to evaluate both our team and our individual players. After doing this for enough years, we have created benchmarks for our team to try to reach on a nightly basis. If we hit our benchmarks, our chance for success is much better.

We have two main offensive strategies that we incorporate and keep track of during games and also during practice:

1) Quality At-Bats

2) B.A.S.E.2.

QUALITY AT-BATS

Players need to shift their perspective from getting hits (which is out of their control) to hitting the ball hard or doing something productive for the team (things they can control). In the QAB System, players have to change the way they evaluate and think about the game that they have played for so many years, but it is to their benefit. In the QAB System players always have a higher QAB average than their regular average and on-base percentage. Typically, a player's QAB average is twice as high as his regular average. In an unfair game, we want to give our players a meaningful way to evaluate their performances, and also to help us make decisions as a coaching staff as to who is really doing the most for our team, throughout the season. The thing that we take into consideration, that no one else does, is productive outs that players make. You should get credit for doing something positive for the team, yet in the calculation of average, your average drops. Even if you sacrifice bunt, your average stays the same and it is not credited for or against you. It is as if it never happened. This is just one example that happens in the game of baseball, where the hitter gets screwed even if he did all he can. The bottom line is that we want to give credit where credit is due. This is why I love the QAB average and throughout the course of the season, as far as numbers go, it is the only thing I post in the dugout or show players on the bus.

WHAT IS A QAB?

There are nine things that a player can do to get credit for QAB:

1) Hard Hit Ball

2) Walk

3) Hit By Pitch

4) Move Runner(s) with No Outs

5) Score Runner From 3rd with Fewer Than Two Outs

6) Base Hit

7) Six Pitch At-Bat Not Ending in a Strikeout

8) Nine Pitch At-Bat Even Ending in a Strikeout

9) Catcher's Interference

We have a chart that we use during games to keep track of how players are doing. This information then goes into a spreadsheet that I created on my iPad which calculates the team average for the night and also keeps a running total for each player.

We use the same QAB system during our practices. When we do hit, it is situational hitting and we evaluate our team on the same nine things. We have a certain QAB percentage that we are trying to hit each night at practice. As we get closer to the season, the percentage starts to climb, and once we are in post-season practice mode, we raise the bar even higher.

After keeping this data for a number of years, I have found that when it comes to QAB percentage as a team, 60% is the number to beat. We keep track of all the same data on JV and varsity. Over the course of five years at Martensdale-St. Mary's, when we were at or above 60%, our overall record for JV/Varsity was 235-10-3. Over the same five-year span, when we are under 60%, our record is 50-25-4. Not terrible, but a far cry from a 95% winning percentage when we are at 60% or above. It has become something to shoot for within our program. It is the game within the game for us. Our players know the theory behind it, and that if we get to 60%, we rarely lose. Nothing is guaranteed, I tell our players, but I like our chances.

I always envied track coaches. They merely time the runners and the fastest make it. They probably do not get too many phone calls or e-mails from the parents of the sixth fastest runner, wondering why he isn't in the relay. Fast is in—it is cut-and-dry. With the QAB system, I take the same approach that the top nine hitters are in. It is factual evidence to support why, or why not, players are in the line-up. There are certain exceptions due to positioning of players, but I would say that 95% of the time, I have the nine highest QAB averages in the line-up. It makes things easy to do and it is not based on a coach's opinion of who is hitting better.

We keep QAB averages during practice, as well. This allows a coach to see who is doing well and deserves to be in the line-up. During practice, we want to evaluate players on the very same scale that we use during the games. It is consistency. If you are measuring the players during the games, saying that this is important to you as a coach and the program, then going the extra step during practice is only going to underscore this concept. We practice for three weeks before our first game so I collect plenty of data to help me make decisions come the first game. You may not have as much practice time which means every at-bat a player takes will be that much more important. As we start practice, our team goal for the practice is to hit 60% QABs and after the first week of practice, it goes to 65%, and so on. I usually throw during our situations, but try to mimic pitchers we will encounter with speed and changing speeds. If the players do not hit at, or above the percentage, then they run three triangles under 1:30 each. That is running from home to the right field foul pole, to the left field foul pole, and then back to home. Depending on how big your field is, this can get pretty difficult for players.

The other big benefit from using a QAB average is that players will begin to see themselves as being more successful. We all know that confidence in baseball is as fragile as a piece of glass. We are talking about high school kids who want to play at the next level and do well every night. It is a no-brainer to me to show a player he is hitting .666 QAB, rather than .350 regular average. Telling a player they are doing something good for the team, two out of every three at-bats, sounds great because it is. Rather than the .350 average, that is a little better than 3 out of 10.

B.A.S.E.2.

The B.A.S.E.2. System is the other offensive philosophy that we use. It is a team concept and not measured on individual performance.

- **Big Inning**

- **Answer Back**

- **Score First**

- **Extend Lead**

- **Score with 2 Outs**

This is just a checklist system that one of our players will use to keep track of during the JV/Varsity games. We all know that scoring runs wins games. What B.A.S.E.2. provides is a premium on how we score runs. I hate to say that scoring one run might be more important than another run throughout the course of a game, but I do believe that is the case. It sounds wrong, but when and how you score runs is critical when it comes to end result. This is another process-based outcome for our players to shoot for during the game. Do these things and, in the end, the results will be there.

The game within the game is to have three of the five check marks by the end of the game.

BIG INNING

A big inning is when you score three or more runs in any inning. You only need to do this once during the course of the game to get that check mark. If you do it multiple times you do not get extra check marks.

ANSWER BACK

Once the other team scores any amount of runs in one half inning, we try to come back in the next half and score. If our opponents score four runs in the top half and we just score one run, then we have cut the lead and killed some of their momentum. Again, this is just needs to be done once during the course of a game—you cannot get more than one check mark per game. The best-case scenario is to get four check marks and shut a team out. Our players always like to joke that they didn't get all five, but it is impossible to answer back when the other team does not score. As your team and coaching staff start to understand the B.A.S.E.2. philosophy, your players will really start to develop an awareness to win. After they have given up some runs on defense, they will come into the dugout and start trying to rally, telling each other to "answer back." At that, point you know your team gets it.

SCORE FIRST

This is self-explanatory but if you score first in the bottom of the fourth inning, then you get the check mark. If you are the home team and allow even one run in the top half of the first inning, then you have given that check mark away and cannot get it back. This is why we really do not mind being visitors, because it gives us the opportunity to score right away, grab that checkmark for sure, and never give the other team the chance.

EXTEND THE LEAD

You get a check mark for having the lead going into your team's turn to bat and scoring even one run to make it even tougher for the other team to get back in it. This is a great one for your team, because once you do have the lead, or maybe have pulled ahead, it does not allow for your team to get complacent and coast in.

It keeps them playing hard, from first pitch to last pitch. Again, one check for accomplishing this, even though you may do it more than once in the course of the game.

SCORE WITH 2 OUTS

The fifth and final check mark that is possible with the B.A.S.E.2. System is to score with two outs. There are some modifications you could make with this one but we have made it as simple as possible. Simply score with two outs and you get the check mark. Some coaches want to do it with just an RBI hit with two outs and that is totally fine. I feel that any time you can get a run across the plate with two outs and the other team so close to ending the inning, it is a huge advantage and momentum swing for your team. So, we give our team credit for scoring with two outs on a pass ball, wild pitch, base hit, error, or any other number of things that could occur with two outs. We put ourselves in a position to score, and even though the other team may have made a mistake, we were able to capitalize on it.

We always aim to get at least three of the five possibilities of B.A.S.E.2. In the time we have been using this philosophy on our JV/Varsity teams, if we get three or more we have been a combined 220-6. It is a staggering statistic when you think about it. That is 97.3% of the time your team is going to win, if you commit to the process and score runs in a certain way, rather than just scoring to score, or without a plan. The funny thing is you can actually get three check marks in the first inning—you can have a big inning, while scoring first, and score with two outs. For us, this has happened from time to time and that is why "Extend the Lead" is great, because you can tell your team they still have other check marks to get. But, the percentage is on your side if you are able to have a three-check mark inning early in the game.

PITCH PHILOSOPHIES/QUALITY INNINGS

When I started using quality at-bats early in my coaching career, I immediately noticed the benefit of having something like that in place for our hitters. What was needed was a way to have the same type of process-based philosophy for our pitchers and the quality inning concept was born. If a hitter can have a quality plate appearance, then a pitcher should be able to have a quality inning. Notice, we are not even talking about a quality outing— just inning-by-inning, batter-by-batter, and pitch-by-pitch. Knowing that if they do have enough winning pitches, they will have a good chance for victory—that is what makes a 1-Pitch Warrior a 1-Pitch Warrior.

A quality inning is when a pitcher throws 13 pitches, or fewer. I settled on 13 pitches, because if a pitcher can do this seven times in a game, then he should have a very good chance of going the distance and pitching a complete game. Obviously, 13 pitches x 7 innings = 91 pitches. I would think that most starters can do this and it is not an unreasonable number of pitches. Even if the pitcher were able to only have four quality innings out of seven, his chances to get to the last inning are going to improve. We know that in high school, especially, what is waiting in the bullpen is usually not going to be as strong as what we see at the beginning of the game.

The quality innings concept puts a premium on a low-pitch count, getting three outs with the fewest number of pitches possible. We do not talk about striking out opposing batters. We stick to the "Simple Wins" philosophy. Baseball is not complicated. If we throw strikes and make plays on defense, we will have a chance to win games. That is what quality innings are all about.

Defense does play a part in whether a pitcher can earn a quality inning, which in some respects, I like and others I do not. When a pitcher is throwing strikes, yet is not getting the support he needs in an inning, he has a tendency to get upset or try harder, something that we definitely try to avoid at all costs. We remind those pitchers to think about what he can control. He is throwing strikes and doing his job. All we ever ask of our pitchers is to throw strikes. That is it. Do not win the game; do not get outs; just throw strikes. The rest is out of their hands.

When the defense is not playing well and making mistakes, errors, or bad decisions that are costing the pitcher a quality inning, then that is something you must address as a team. You need to remind them of your philosophies. Defense must work together with the pitcher to earn quality innings. It is not just the sole responsibility of the pitcher to earn a quality inning—it is a collective effort of the entire defense. Quality innings are a team concept, much like the B.A.S.E.2. on offense, when you really think about it.

Our quality inning chart includes other things that we keep track of that I think are pretty standard in most programs, but maybe not. We are assessing a pitcher's first pitch strike % and overall strike % and then, as the inning comes to a close, we determine if a Quality Inning should be awarded. A player on the bench, usually another pitcher, is responsible for doing the pitching chart, as well. I have found it helps players stay in the game and learn the philosophies of the team. Having a player keep the chart means I do not have to worry about it during the game, but I can check with the player for pitch count if I am concerned about the number of pitches a player has thrown.

Just like with QABs and B.A.S.E.2., we have certain benchmarks we want pitchers to hit. With first pitch strike % and overall strike %, we want our pitchers to be at or above 60%. For Quality Innings we want pitchers/team to be around 50%.

A3P – AFTER THREE PITCHES

Another way we monitor a pitcher's performance is something called A3P, which means "After 3 Pitches." We have a player in the dugout keep a chart for this, too, because data do not lie. Measurement equals motivation. A big part of what we do is collecting data. It is the basis for making decisions and helping players. For a pitcher to earn an A3P, he has to have one of two things happen:

1) Have a batter put the ball in play within the first three pitches.

2) Have a one ball and two strike count on the batter.

If one of these two does not happen, then the pitcher loses the chance to get an A3P for that batter and will reset on the next hitter. I really like this tool as a way to measure the pitcher solely on what he can control, as it does not factor in the defense, at all. It is also a great way for pitchers to work on getting ahead in counts and doing what we preach—throw strikes!!! A3P is a great measure for pitchers, too, because we do not want a player thinking that because he did not throw a first pitch strike, that he is screwed. A pitcher could throw a ball on the first pitch and come back with two strikes and win the A3P. It also ties in to the 1-Pitch Warrior Mentality, because pitchers are trying to win small increments and not the entire game. If he does not get an A3P for the last hit, we "flush it" and move on to the next hitter. We get focused with our routine and play the next pitch!

We are trying to get an A3P two out of every three batters, or 66.6%. Again, this benchmark works with the idea that getting outs, while keeping pitch count low, is what we are after. All this data help my coaching staff and me make decisions on who is more effective, who is our number 1, 2, and so on, as we move into the post-season. The numbers do not lie.

Keeping this data also has an added benefit for pitchers. As mentioned earlier, baseball is a brutally unfair game. Pitching is no different than hitting. You can have a good outing and get nothing to show for it. You pitch your rear off, but the bats are alive that night, or the defense makes some costly errors. Most pitchers are going to want to take the blame for the loss, because that is how it looks in the stats and they are competitors, but is a totally unfair way to look at a pitching performance as either good or bad. No pitching performance is good or bad. It is good AND bad. What these stats, like A3P, first pitch strike %, strike % and quality innings do, is to really get down to how a pitcher performed that night, without taking into consideration the outcome of the game. Looking at solely the things the pitcher could control, is the only way you should look at your pitchers. The wins and strikeouts will come if they commit to the system.

We had a pitcher name J.D. Nielsen who was at the losing end of things early in the year. He was the starting pitcher for our game against Des Moines East when we had a chance to tie the national record for consecutive wins with 89. We lost 4-3...SO WHAT, NEXT PITCH! In J.D.'s next start, we faced a pitcher named Colin Thomas who dominated our hitters and struck out 15; we lost 2-1. Obviously, not the way any pitcher wants to start the year. But, I had a talk with him after those two starts, showing him the numbers on his performance, making sure he realized that he was doing everything he could and everything we asked of our pitchers. I showed him that all of his percentages were at or above the benchmarks. He needed to gain confidence from those starts, rather than let them eat him up. He had a choice to either get better or get bitter. J.D. pitched great the rest of the year, choosing to get better, and he did. He ended up starting the championship game for us in 2012 and he pitched the game of his life, beating Mason City Newman 1-0, and in the process, throwing a no-hitter. He was completely locked in and competed to win every pitch, regardless of the previous pitch. He was the definition of a 1-Pitch Warrior that day. He played his best when it mattered most and I could not have been prouder of how much he had matured as a player, not so much physically as mentally.

If you are interested in the charts, spreadsheets, practice plans, or more 1-Pitch Warrior ideas that we use within our program, please check out www.1PitchWarrior.com for the 1-Pitch Warrior System. It goes into even more detail than is covered in this book. Other CDs and merchandise is available, also.

TEAM PROCESS INDEX (TPI)/WHY TPI?

Team Process Index is a calculation that is based on a team's performance, using key indicators that, in and of themselves, are very revealing in determining a team's chance to win. TPI is a new and innovative way to measure the things that matter most. It shows how efficient a team has been during the game and will show strengths and weaknesses, not only in a single game, but also in patterns throughout the season. It is based on process goals. TPI operates with the premise that if players consistently do certain things well, they will maximize their team's chances to win. What TPI does is plan the work; now, you have to work the plan!

We all know that one of four things will happen once the first pitch is thrown:

1) You will play well and win.

2) You will play well and lose.

3) You will play poorly and win.

4) You will play poorly and lose.

Using a TPI to truly evaluate play regardless of wins and losses is a better way of creating an environment of improvement. It helps a team move past the simple happiness of a win, to focus on finding things to improved upon for the next game, so that your team has an even better chance of victory. If you focus only on results, you can get lost in the thrill of victory, being satisfied with what may have been a sub-par performance. Using the Team Process Index prevents this. It creates a dynamic of constructive criticism that will encourage growth within any program, at any level.

WHAT MAKES UP THE TPI?

There are 10 Key Indicators:

1) Error Differential

2) Walks/HBP Differential

3) Strikeout Differential

4) Stolen Base Differential

The B.A.S.E.2. System makes up indicators 5 thru 9:

5) Big Inning

6) Answer Back

7) Score 1st

8) Extend the Lead

9) Score with 2 Outs

10) The Quality At-Bat System

These criteria have been selected because they are measures of efficiency in all facets—pitching, defense, base-running, offense—of the game.

B.A.S.E.2. is a great indicator, in and of itself. Since the implementation of the B.A.S.E.2. System, our team has been 220-6 once we mastered three of the five categories in B.A.S.E.2.

QABs are a great indicator, too. Since we began measuring our QAB % for each game, we have been 235-10-2 when we are above 60%, while only 50-25-4 when having a QAB % under 60%.

The bad part about using only the QAB/B.A.S.E.2. Systems is the fact that they are completely offensive measurements. We wanted to come up with something more comprehensive and also more reliable than just B.A.S.E.2. and QAB. Even though they are good, TPI is rock solid!

HOW TO CALCULATE TPI?

Each category is given a point value in the TPI system. After looking at past seasons and the data we have collected thus far, we have found that a TPI above 48 points predicted a winning outcome 98.75% of the time. The best part is that we did not factor our 88-game win streak into the calculations. We wanted it to stand alone without those number-inflating factors. On the other end of things, when teams were below 48 points, their winning percentage was just above .500. Again, we are not after the results-only things within the process. The point is, if you do these things correctly, then success may come your way. Winning is a byproduct of working this process. TPI can be a way to focus your entire program and communicate team philosophy.

We have created an easy-to-use worksheet for coaches to calculate TPI. The analysis is so easy that it can be done in just a few minutes after each game as you look over the scorebook. This data can be used to debrief your team after a game, which most coaches already do. You can now make this meeting more productive and go over facts, rather than just rant about your feelings and how play was "poor" or "great." Would it not make more sense to tell your team the specific things they either did, or did not do, that contributed to the game's outcome? I am not insulting any coach's intelligence by saying that individual players are not going to know what went well overall during the course of the game. TPI gives teams a much more systematic way of reacting to their own performance, because it is fact-driven. The numbers do not lie. Praise your team when their TPI is high, or they have set a season record. Give them positive, constructive criticism when things do not go well with TPI, as well.

WHEN?

Start now! Why not use TPI? Remember: This not a way to win more games. It is a way to provide feedback to players and coaches. Such constructive criticism will help you continue to make strides in becoming the best team possible. Let the data drive your decisions rather than rely on subjective feelings that often get in the way and are not helpful. With TPI, stay focused on the process and not the end result.

Visit www.1pitchwarrior.com/extras
for BONUS 1-Pitch Warrior Tips
& FREE Systems of Success

1-PW POINTS FOR REVIEW:

- **Using measurements on what a player can truly control is only fair to your players.**

- **Measurements, such as QABs, Quality Innings and A3P, allow players to see progress and also gain confidence even in defeat.**

- **Systems win!**

NOTES:

www.1pitchwarrior.com

NOTES:

CHAPTER 4: 1-PITCH WARRIOR MENTALITY

Next are phrases, acronyms, and quotes that we use to talk with our players about being a 1-Pitch Warrior. This shared vocabulary will help coaches and players understand all the facets of the 1-Pitch Warrior Mentality and can be used as a quick daily-read for players, or coaches can use their favorites as practice starters. We call them skull sessions or mental minutes. It does not take long to talk about them, but they serve as constant reminders. We have been doing this for years—it does not hurt to remind the players how they got where they are today.

Other ideas could be to use these in e-mails, tweets, or texts to your players. Any way to help your players understand the mental side of the game is a great way to use this next section. We have taken many of these sayings and created posters for our players to hang in our gym and our dugout. Remember, we want to advertise all the time.

DEVELOPING THE 1-PITCH WARRIOR MENTALITY

As found in the book *Heads Up Baseball* by Tom Hanson and Ken Ravizza there are Two Rules of the Mental Game:

1) You have very little control of what goes on around you.

2) You have total control of how you respond to it.

Players need to fully understand this statement before moving on to anything else. They have to learn that striking out, making an error, or making a bad decision is not the end. Those are just events and they choose to assign meaning to them. They either continue to self-destruct because of how they respond, or get back to playing one-pitch-at-a-time, which will always give them the best chance for success. The teams that win the most games are the ones that understand that what happened is over and done. Pressing on and working to win the next pitch is all they can do. Play for the present.

ACT DIFFERENTLY FROM HOW YOU FEEL

It is a guarantee that there will be days when your players or coaches do not feel their best. They may be tired from the long road trip the night before, or from work. They may be hungry, have had a fight at home, earned a low score on a test, etc. The thing that we all can understand and agree on is we usually play our best when we feel good. So the question is, how do we get players to change their feelings from not so great to good or great? How you feel is your choice. Remember the two Rules of Mental Game: how they respond is a choice. All we have to do is choose the alternative. It is that simple, but most players do not have that built-in skill set yet. I believe that being mentally tough is a skill that all players and people can learn. Just like fielding a groundball or hitting a curveball, players can develop the awareness and mental skills required to be a 1-Pitch Warrior, always putting their best foot forward regardless of how they feel.

Actions your players can take on a daily basis to work on mental toughness and act differently from how they feel are:

1) **Get up out of bed when the alarm goes off. No questions asked.**
2) **Make your bed.**
3) **Brush your teeth before bed and when you wake.**
4) **Shave daily.**
5) **Buckle your seat belt every time you get in the car.**

6) Do not text and drive

These are things that are not hard, but how many of your players do these on a daily basis? Practicing these routines will allow them to understand what it means to act differently from how they feel, because most of them will not want to do these simple tasks. Remember: Mental toughness can be trained. It is just a matter of knowing how.

MEASUREMENT = MOTIVATION

As you can see, our practices and games revolve around collecting data and measuring our performances based on numbers, not opinions. There is no doubt that players will run harder when you have a stopwatch than when you do not. Put a time on your infielders and make them get the ball to first under that time and watch what happens. Create an All-Time Best List for QABs in a game, season, best %, team best, etc. Make a point that this is what matters. Hold your players to certain standards in practice, and if they don't get it done, then make them run or do something as a consequence for not meeting your expectations. Measure what matters to you and hold players accountable. Also hold yourself accountable to calculate the data and post them in your dugout so players can see the results. If you never show them, then the players will think it does not matter. Another idea that I think will go a long way in letting your players know what matters in your program, is to give them the end-of-the-year statistics for QABs and the pitching stats, as well. To take it a step further, you can have a quality at-bat champ and give awards for any other stats that you feel are worthy.

PLAY VS. YOURSELF AND THE GAME

Augie Garrido, Head Baseball Coach at The University of

Texas, said that the game of baseball has two major challenges that make things extremely difficult— boredom and frustration. The game of baseball will deal you a hand you do not want to play on a nightly basis. Things will not go your way. Adversity is a common occurrence and learning to overcome the frustration is the difference between getting out of a big inning, or letting that inning make a difference. A 1-Pitch Warrior knows how to battle adversity by refocusing and releasing in order to get back to winning the next pitch; by slowing the game down; using his routines; and increasing his focus on the things he can do to change the current situation. Boredom is easy to overcome with solid routines. It is all right to space out when the play is over, but defensively stepping into the circle of control or concentration will always allow you to get back to a ready-to-react mode.

CONFIDENCE IS A CHOICE

No one can take confidence away from someone without his permission. Because you are not in the line-up that day, should not shatter your confidence. If you went 0-4 the night before has nothing to do with how you will perform tonight, unless you let it. Always walk to the plate or mound with your chest out, knowing that you can get it done. Being a 1-Pitch Warrior does not mean you will always win and that everything will go your way. It means responding with your best in the face of adversity and always playing with confidence. Do not let anyone deflate your confidence. Confidence must be bulletproof. The problem most players have is that they let past performance dictate future outcomes. The past in no way plays a part in what will happen at this moment.

GOOD OR BAD VS. GOOD AND BAD

Players almost always evaluate how they have played as either good or bad. They are very hard on themselves and they view it as black or white. Even if they made a nice play in the outfield, but went 0 for 4 at the plate, most would say they played badly. This is a big perspective shift for them. They cannot personalize performance. They need to understand that, even when things are going great, there is still bad mixed in and vice versa. We won 88 games in a row, which was amazing, and people think everything must have been perfect for us to do that. That could not be further from the truth. There were many games in which we made errors, walked hitters, struck out, etc. We were able to play better than the opponent for 88 games in a row, but to say it was all good in "The Streak" would be a lie. You can even wish your team a good-bad day, because it always will be both. It is what we choose to focus on that we will remember. After games, coaches need to honestly evaluate how things went and ask, "What went well?" and "What went badly?"

FAILURE IS NEVER FINAL

When adversity comes your way, either with a bad call or the final outcome of a game, remember that failure is never final. Quitters never start, losers never finish, and winners never stop. You will get knocked down, but those who get back up are the ones who will succeed. You must learn to view failure as positive feedback. If you are losing and having to struggle, then you probably are not getting any better. Learn from your mistakes and, when you lose, choose to learn.

PERFECTION VS. EXCELLENCE

There is no such thing as perfection this side of heaven. If you expect to be perfect every night, then you need to stop lying to yourself. You are setting yourself up for disappointment. No one lives up to being perfect. Hall of Famers hit over .300 for their careers. That means they were nowhere near perfect. They were out more than the number of hits they collected throughout their careers. Get over perfect! Instead, think about excellence. Eighty-eight wins in a row and three straight state titles did not come from trying to be perfect. It came from trying to be excellent on a nightly basis. During BP, practice, and extra hours invested, we understood that excellence is not an event; it is a lifestyle. Holding championship trophies at the end of the season does not come without the journey of hours, upon hours, of work to make it happen.

REARVIEW MIRROR VS. WINDSHIELD

God gave us eyes in the front of our head for a reason—to keep pressing on and moving forward. The past is history; the future is a mystery; we call it the present, because it is a gift. Looking back on past pain will only give you more of the same. Focusing on the present, with all our effort and concentration, allows us to enjoy the moment and gives us an opportunity to play our best. Look ahead through the windshield to the next pitch and never back through the rearview.

GET BETTER OR GET BITTER

If you lose you have two choices: to get better or bitter. Many people choose the second option and point fingers, blame others, and make excuses for what happened. A 1-Pitch Warrior rises above all of that by living above the line, accepting responsibility for what happened, assessing the situation with a clear mind, and moving on with the intent to get better. A 1-Pitch Warrior uses the loss as a catalyst to something bigger and better. Remember that any fool can criticize and most do.

THE BEST TEAM NEVER WINS

Most people will say that the best team always wins. I disagree. The team that plays better always wins. Many teams look better on paper, have more talent, or more tradition, but none of that matters once the first pitch is thrown. Everyone has lost a game they felt they deserved to win hands down, or has watched the big upset on TV. It happens all the time. You don't have to be better than the other team; you just have to play better. That is why we prepare and work so hard. Practice does not make perfect. Practice makes permanent. Every time we step on the field, we always want to give our team the best chance to play better than the other team.

HAVE TO VS. GET TO

We have talked a lot about perspective throughout what it means to be a 1-Pitch Warrior and "have to vs. want to" is another step to gaining the correct perspective on things. Many players and even coaches may get to the day when they say I "have to" go to practice. I tell players there are no "have to" guys in our program. I do not make anyone come and no one is forced by anyone to be there. Then, I remind them that the door always opens in both directions. As my friend Brian Cain would say, "It is welcoming you in to dominate the day!" or, if you don't "want" to be there, then you are free to leave at any point.

Simply put, I want players who want to be there, who enjoy the game, and understand the time it takes to be excellent at it. If your attitude is "have to" instead of "want to," then you will not get the most out of your potential. In addition, you are hurting others around you. Players have left our program, or not gone out because they understand this principle and how much it means to me as a coach.

A player that has a "have to" attitude is a drain on the program. A player that has a "get to" attitude is an asset to your program. He understands that he gets to be a part of something special. He gets to play a sport he loves in a country that is free. Although he has the right perspective, we want this player to take things one step further. We want him to turn his "get to" into "want to."

It is much more powerful to say, "I want to go to practice today" than saying something like, "I have to go to practice." Evaluate yourself on where you are on the have/get/want scale. Then, change the way you talk to yourself on the days you catch yourself saying things like, "I have to do this homework assignment," or "I have to go lift weights." Those who want to are those who win!

TURN PRESSURE INTO PLEASURE (BEING COMFORTABLE WITH THE UNCOMFORTABLE)

Let's face it. Sports are pressure-packed. When the game is on the line, will you be mentally ready so you can focus on what really matters? Or, will you be distracted by the crowd noise, the other team's dugout, visions of failure, thoughts of winning, or past experiences that didn't go your way? You must train yourself to stay calm. Your biggest weapon against a tough spot is breathing. We must be focused. Breathing, a focal point, and task-oriented thoughts—trust your routine. Two other great ways to make sure you are ready for anything when your number is called in the game of your life are 1) putting yourself in tough situations at practice and 2) using imagery and visualization to create tough situations for yourself before they ever happen. These are dress rehearsals for the real things. Although nothing can ever simulate the real thing, these practices go a long way in developing the faith in yourself to get it done, because you were able to do it at practice and also in your own mind.

THE MENTAL BRICK

The stress of living in the past will weigh anyone down. Sports are no different especially because of all the hours athletes invest on the field to be great. We are competitors, but at times, we carry the missed opportunities, errors, strikeouts, and losses with us. We carry our past around with us until the next at-bat, or maybe even take it home with us. Then, we show up to the field the next day with our bad experiences. A brick is what those frustrating moments feel like, as we are unable to get over them. We dwell on those situations instead of developing a way to deal with them. They weigh us down, to the point that you can actually see it. Physical body language says, "I am in a slump," or "I'm disappointed with my performance." Players get the loser limp, because they cannot get rid of the mental brick. Put the real brick in your back pocket. Can you play at your best with the brick? Your thoughts will slow you down in the same way!

SO WHAT, NEXT PITCH

After realizing that our thoughts are powerful enough to slow us down, then the next question should be: how do I get rid of the mental brick? It is an easy concept to understand, but with players' thoughts, sometimes it is tough to do anything about them. Coaches say things like, "get over it," "forget about it," "you're fine," etc. All of these platitudes just don't work when we are already frustrated. Players need to train themselves to combat their negative thoughts with one main thought… "So What, Next Pitch." It is all about realizing that you need to play the game as a 1-Pitch Warrior. Once players realize that they need a change, that is when they must slow the game down. Take extra time, find a focal point, get a deep breath, and replace the negative thoughts that are performance killers with ones that can help them get back on track as soon as possible. The last thought is so important. It needs to be task-oriented, such as "see the ball big," "hit the glove," but not thoughts like "don't swing at a curve," "don't strike out," etc. The mind does not seem to know the difference between do and do not. For example, if I told you, "Don't think about wearing purple shoes," it would not stop you from actually looking at your feet and visualizing purple shoes. In fact, it creates an awareness about purple shoes—the very thing I did not want you to do. In baseball, we do the same thing. If our self-talk is "don't strike out" or "don't miss this groundball," it is as if we are actually telling ourselves to go ahead and mess up. This is where we must train our minds to think about the things we want to do, rather the things we want to avoid. There is a big difference between the two. Thoughts need to be task-oriented. This will steer you toward enhancing your performance and not killing it before you even have the opportunity.

MOTION OVER EMOTION

Keep going. Do not stop because you do not "feel" well. We are not trying to create robots that have no feelings and just go through the motions. That is not at all what we want. But, we want players to understand that there are going to be days that do not feel right or great. It does not mean that you cannot play great and come out on top. During the course of the season, it is inevitable that you will feel amazing on some days, but after your fourth or fifth game of the week, you probably will not feel so amazing. Do not succumb to the emotions that are saying "I can't pitch well today," "I am too tired," "I can't hit today," or "I feel slow." Remember to "fake it, 'til you make it." I believe that this is where many slumps begin. Act differently from how you feel and give yourself an opportunity to be at your best. On the days you do not feel your best, do not make excuses; take action and act like a .400 hitter even though you might only feel like a .200 hitter

PROCESS OVER OUTCOME

This is one of the main principles of a 1-Pitch Warrior. We must focus on what we can control in the present moment. Many players want a great pitching record, or a great batting average. There is nothing wrong with that, but they forget about how those things actually come to pass. The only way to have a great season on the mound and a solid record is not to strike guys out. It is not even to get outs. Those are by-products of only one thing—throwing strikes! Pitchers, listen closely: you will be better if you focus on the only thing that you can control, which is getting the ball over the plate. Even when you do, sometimes it will not be called a strike. Remember there is no such thing as a strike zone, only an umpire zone. So What, Next Pitch. Do not go out to the mound thinking about winning or losing. Think about competing every pitch and making quality pitches. Quality pitches lead to quality innings, and quality innings lead to quality outings, which, unfortunately in baseball, still do not mean that you will win. This is a brutal game. Grasp that fact and the fact that if you commit to each pitch and do a good job throwing strikes consistently, then you are giving your team its best chance for the win. The rest is out of your hands.

Hitting is much the same. You do not just magically hit .300. Obviously you must get hits, but getting a hit boils down to one thing: putting a good swing on a good pitch. Again, even then you are not guaranteed the desired outcome. This is why you should evaluate yourself on the process and not on the end result. End result is a trap, especially as difficult as baseball is. It can be even more difficult when you do not work the process. Have faith and trust that if you work the process, take good swings, and make good pitches, then all that other stuff will come.

The final goal for many teams will be a conference championship or maybe a state title. There is nothing wrong with setting goals. Goals are great. The problem is that most people make them and then forget about them or do not work the process to achieve them. An example is a student who sets a goal of getting an A in a class, and then does not do homework or study before quizzes or tests. It makes no sense to set goals if you do not have process-based goals to go along with them. We get too focused on the end goal instead of working the little things we can do today. Done repeatedly, these little things will get you where you want to go. Set small goals along the way. The student could say, "I am going to turn in all assignments this week," or "I am going to go to tutoring twice this week." These are things they control and will also help achieve the bigger goal of earning the A. Big goals have a funny way of working themselves out when we take care of the small things on consistent basis. Do not get so wrapped up in trying to earn the A that you forget about what it takes to earn it. Take each day 200 feet at a time. Some days you may have to take each day one breath at a time to work your way through it. What is the best way to eat an elephant? One bite at a time! The most amazing things can be accomplished with a great deal of concentrated effort and knowing that it will not come overnight.

WILL OVER SKILL

Did you know that in Major League Baseball, 55% of the home games are won? Theoretically, there is no more chance of winning at home than on the road. You have equal opportunity. This is just one of many examples of "will over skill." I always use the example of nine players who are great, but play for themselves, or nine good players playing for each other. Who would you pick? In my opinion, the nine great players are playing against 10, because the good team has a 10th man called determination and faith. You cannot rely solely on your physical talent, because there will come a time that your opponent has exactly what you have. The difference makers will be your mental toughness and your passion. I can say from experience that heads and hearts win the hard ones more times than not.

TBT (THOUGHTS BECOME THINGS)

There is a simple idea that we get what we think most about. Before any amazing revolutionary invention was created, it had to start as someone's idea. Cars did not just drop down out of the sky; computers were not a gift from above. The gift that we are given from above is the amazing ability to dream big things and to know that they are possible. Whether it was the first airplane, TV, iPad, cell phone, or space shuttle launch, it took a great deal of courage to see it through from beginning to end. Knowing that it has not been done before takes faith in yourself when others will doubt you. You must believe. You must fake it 'til you make it. Thoughts produce actions. Long before any champions are crowned, they had to act like champions and do the things that champions do. That is the beauty of it. You do not even have to be a champion to start acting like one. You just need to think like one. Like attracts like. Think about being a champion and you just might be. The more you do, the more you are likely to do what is necessary to see something that was once never there, or that you have never done before.

THE 86,400 PRINCIPLE (SPEND VS. INVEST)

What if I told you a destination that you dream of awaits you, and each day, you were only able to take 86,400 steps toward that destination? At the end of the day, any steps that were not taken are wiped clean and cannot be used the following day. In addition, the next day you woke up, you would receive 86,400 new steps to use as you please. What direction would you go as you embarked on the journey? I imagine that most of us would take steps directly toward where we want to go. In all reality, this is the opportunity that all of us have every day. We all have goals and ambitions, on and off the field of play. Our destinations include graduating college, getting in the starting line-up, owning a business, or any of a million other things. Every day, we are credited with 86,400 seconds to use as we see fit. Time is the most precious thing that anyone has in this world. Some say that time is money. I could not disagree more. You can always earn more money. You can never earn back time that is lost. If you have a goal in mind, whether it is a team goal or an individual one, time is going to play a part in reaching that goal. It may mean that it happens later than expected, or never at all.

Remember that you are only able to use the 86,400 steps somehow today, or they are gone at the end of the day. Some will utilize all of the steps in a very effective and useful manner; some may stray from the course; and some will not use any steps at all in the journey toward their destination. You can take or spend those steps, which may help a little, or you can invest those steps in getting better or closer to where you want to be. Spending can be productive, but may have marginal return. On the other hand, if the limited amount of steps you were about to take today were invested in a cause, think how much more you would get in return. The reward may be greater than ever expected. Your goal may happen faster, or at least have a better chance of coming to pass. There are no guarantees in life, but the amount of time you get each day is a certainty. How you use it is up to you.

THERMOSTAT VS. THERMOMETER

There are players on every team who can create excitement by getting others to respond to adversity or a tough game. They help others have the 1-Pitch Warrior Mentality, remind others to flush it, or tell a teammate "So What, Next Pitch," when they need little extra guidance. They are Thermostats—those who are able to change the atmosphere and attitude of a team and increase the fire and desire that comes from within, not only themselves, but for others around them. Then there are the Thermometers. They just take the temperature and are unable to change with the things that come their way during the course of a game, or a season. They let the situation control them instead of the other way around. These are the players you have played with or against for years. You know that once the going gets tough, they will break and fold. No mental toughness. They are not 1-Pitch Warriors. These are the kind of players you love to play against. Make sure you and those around you are able to heat it up when needed, but also be able to play it cool when things get hectic.

DON'T CONFUSE ACTIVITY WITH PRODUCTIVITY

Often being busy does not lead to the result we want. You put time in, and at the end of the day, you are exhausted from running around like a chicken with your head cut off , but feel as if you barely accomplished anything. It is not the amount of time you put in, but what you put into the time. Fierce focus and dogged tenacity for two hours can often lead to more than eight hours of the routine and the mundane. You need to take each part of practice seriously enough to make it productive. Avoid the temptation to go through the motions. This will undoubtedly lead you, and possibly your team, to be average. Mediocrity is not something I imagine you want or you would not be reading this book. Again, apply some of the techniques in this book to help you stay in the moment. Working with a purpose will lead to a productive drill at practice, to a productive practice, and ultimately, to a productive season.

COMPARED TO WHAT?

The darkest hour is only 60 minutes. You are in the slump of your life. You could not hit water if you fell out of a boat. You have been benched for an underclassman. It seems like you can do nothing right. We have all been there. The world seems like it is coming down around you. You are not just carrying a mental brick—you have an entire truck of them ready to build the Mental Brick Asylum. You are going crazy because you are personalizing your performance. Two things to remember when going through a slump or tough time:

1)   Baseball is what you do; it is not who you are.

2)   The darkest hour is only 60 minutes.

You may think things are terrible, but is going 0 for 10 really that bad? When you are struggling, ask yourself, "Compared to what?" Is losing a few games as bad as losing a teammate? Compared to what? You can always think of some situation that is definitely worse than your on-field play. Keep things in perspective and understand that playing baseball is a beautiful opportunity. You could be fighting in a war; you could be confined to a wheelchair; be homeless; be broke; or even worse, dead. Enjoy the time you have now, before the sands of time in your career hourglass are gone.

TRY VS. WILL

You ask two friends to come over to help you with a task of any sort.

These are their responses:

1st Friend: I'll try to come.

2nd Friend: I will come.

Which friend can you count on?

The answer is simple. Your 2nd friend is the one who will most likely be there to help out. This is a simple example to illustrate something that, at times, goes completely unnoticed. Self-talk plays a large part in the way we feel about ourselves, which in turn can have a huge impact on the way we handle situations and how productive we are. There are many times when you tell yourself, "I will try," much like the friends in the example. Saying you will "try" is almost like a disclaimer; like saying it is all right to fail at a task. It gives you an out in the end to say, "Oh well, I tried." Telling yourself instead that, "I will," or "I can," are statements of commitment. They say to others, and to yourself, that you have faith in the mission at hand. Impossible is only limited by our imagination. Self-talk can play an instrumental part in making it happen. What team do you want to be on? The team that says, "I can try to win the (insert goal here)." Or, the team that says "I can and I will!"

SUCCESS AND WINNING COME FROM THE 6 SWs

Some Will. Some Won't. So What. Stick With It. Someone's Watching. Simple Wins. Champions will do what it takes. Mediocre teams will not. Develop a plan, establish goals within your program, trust in one another, and stick with the plan. Coaches, scouts, fans, community members, family—someone is always watching. This is not a hard game to understand, but we sometimes make a difficult game to play even tougher by not playing it one-pitch-at-a-time. Consistent mind control will result in body control. Whoever can catch, throw, hit, and run the bases the best that day will most likely win. Keep it super simple.

DOn't walT

There have been many different 1-Pitch Warrior Mentality tips in this section and this is the culmination of them all. The time is here. The place is now! There is no substitute for your actions. Invest in your 86,400 seconds every day! If you do not, then someone else will!

 Visit www.1pitchwarrior.com/extras
for BONUS 1-Pitch Warrior Tips
& FREE Systems of Success

1-PW POINTS FOR REVIEW:

- **Create a common language in your program.**

- **Speak to your team about the mental side of the game daily.**

- **Mental toughness is something players can learn.**

NOTES:

NOTES:

www.1pitchwarrior.com

NOTES:

CHAPTER 5: 1-PITCH WARRIOR ACRONYMS OF SUCCESS

F.O.C.U.S. – Follow One Course Until Successful

Success always leaves clues. The players/programs that invest the most are usually the ones that have the best chance at the end of the season. It is no secret. The fact is that most will not follow the path to success. Most will never begin, because quite often, it is the start that stops most people. Those that do start, often fall along the way and never get back on track. The path to greatness is a long one and only a few will truly understand that there is no end to excellence. Work the process like there is no end in sight. There are no traffic jams on the extra mile.

D.W.Y.S.Y.W.D. – Do What You Say You Will Do

The one thing that drives coaches crazy is the player who says, "I know, I know." If you know, then show what you know. Otherwise we would not need to ride your butt for doing it the wrong way. You say you want to be a part of something great? Then, be great. Be great not only during BP, but also during a simple soft-toss drill, or on the 1,000th fly ball you have taken this year off of a coach's fungo. If you are going to talk about it, then be about it.

A.C.E. – Acting Changes Everything

This goes back to acting differently from how you feel. You will not show up to the field every day feeling great or having your best day. That is okay. It is unrealistic to think that you will. The thing you must do is act like you do have your best curve, even though you might not. Despite how you feel, you must still compete with the same tenacity and not give the edge to the competition. If you are tired, that is okay. Just do not act tired. If you are in a slump, that is fine. Just do not act like you are in a slump, or the chance of you staying in the slump will be likely and be a performance killer. Act like you are the best hitter all day and you might just be surprised at what happens. Act "as if."

F.A.I.L. – First Attempt In Learning

The thing about success is that most people see a person's accomplishment after they have discovered or done something great. We do not see the "before," with all the hours of hard work, let downs, second tries, and third tries it took to get where they are today. Remember that failure is necessary for the learning process. The story is that it took Thomas Edison nearly a thousand tries to invent the light bulb. He said, "I have not failed 1,000 times. I have successfully discovered a 1,000 ways to not make a light bulb." The take-away is his perspective on it and also his ability to continue in the face of adversity. Keep reaching, keep pressing on— it is those moments of failure when learning takes place.

W.I.N. – What's Important Now

Understanding the answer to What's Important Now? is key in mental training to become a 1-Pitch Warrior. The only thing that matters during the course of the game is the present moment and the pitch that is coming. We allow our minds to wander, our fear to paralyze us, and our anger to get in the way. We do not want to get analysis paralysis. This is a great question to ask yourself during the course of the game, especially when things are speeding up and getting hectic. This question can help center and refocus your thoughts and get you back to playing the game the only way it should be played—one-pitch-at-a-time!

A.P.E. – Attitude, Perspective, Effort

These are the three things for which you can hold yourself and your players accountable. Win or lose, if you have a great attitude, a good perspective on things, and make an all-out effort, you never lose. You may be upset and disappointed for a bit, but there is always comfort that comes from knowing you did all that was within your power. Coaches, win or lose, try sticking to these three things when evaluating your team on how they played and practiced on any given night. If you are not controlling your A.P.E., then how can you honestly expect to beat quality competition?

G.A.S. – Give A Shoot

We use the analogy of building a fire within our program. A fire needs fuel to burn and to get bigger. Our players provide the G.A.S. during practice. With every rep they take, the fire grows bigger and bigger until the end of the year approaches and it is a raging inferno. Every player is committed to making the fire burn hotter and hotter every day. The only things that can withstand the intensity of a fire are metals, like the metal found in championship rings. How big will your fire be this season? How much G.A.S. will you put on the fire?

B.I.G. – Breathe In Greatness

We all want to play big in the big game. We are competitors who dream of those types of moments. Many times, however, we stumble once we get our chance or do not quite live up to our expectations. John Wooden said it best, "The more concerned we become over things we can't control, the less we will do with the things we can control." Make "Getting B.I.G." one of your staples. Most would say that baseball is a slow game, and it is, compared to other sports. But, for those who have stepped on the diamond, before you know it, the game can feel like it is moving at a million miles an hour. When things speed up on you, you now have a technique to go to. You Get B.I.G. Take a slow, controlled, deep breath and blow it out slowly. This is what was mentioned earlier as part of your routine. But even then, there might be times when an extra second is needed. This is your go-to. This is how in the face of adversity 1-Pitch Warriors respond.

A.B.C. – Act Big, Breathe Big, Commit Big

This acronym comes straight from the title of Tom Hanson's book, *Act Big, Breathe Big, Commit Big*. This is another great way to sum up what it means to be a 1-Pitch Warrior. It includes all of what has been outlined in this book. Acting big with confidence, even when you don't feel your best. Breathing big, when the pressure is on. Learning to slow the game down and have a focal point to go to, when you need it. Trusting your routine to help you to live in the moment and focus all your attention on winning this pitch. Committing big to the next 200 feet and the process of getting better in small increments. Not looking too far ahead, or in the rearview. Remember your ABCs so you can play your best when it matters most.

A.B.C. – Always Behave Confidently

Confidence is a choice. Playing without confidence is like going to a duel without bullets in your gun. For every pitch there will be a winner and a loser. If you go into a pitch without confidence to win it, are you giving yourself the best chance to come out of that moment victorious? Winning games are the outcomes of winning moments. You cannot give up those moments because you lack confidence. You have invested too much time not to be confident. Do not let a coach, parent, umpire, or opponent take your confidence away. It is yours. Protect it and you will be that much closer to your goal.

P.R.I.D.E. – Personal Responsibility In Daily Excellence

This sums up what mental toughness is all about. It is up to you. It is your responsibility to give what you can, day in and day out. Your coach and teammates can only push you so far, and in the end, it is your decision to work for excellence, or to give less then your best. You may be able to fool other people, but you cannot fool yourself. You are the one who has to live with the effort that you give. You either look yourself in the mirror, knowing you did everything you could at practice to help yourself and the team get better, or you fall short. Win or lose, you always will feel satisfied with the day, if you have invested well. There is nothing more gratifying than knowing you did your best.

H.A.T.E.R.S. – Having Anger Toward Everyone Reaching Success

Along the way, people will always question, scrutinize, and criticize much, if not all of what you do, and how you do it. I always hold to two simple statements here:

1) Those that matter, do not mind and those who mind, do not matter.

2) Any fool can criticize and most do.

Lead the ways you see best and do not worry what others will think or what they might say. It does not matter. There are speed bumps along the journey. Roll right over them and keep pressing on.

R.I.N.G.S. – Realizing It Never Gets Sweeter

It is what every baseball player dreams of—winning the last game they play. Tossing that helmet, glove, whatever may be near in the air, and hopping on the dog pile. It is pure joy! It is the moment you begin to understand that getting to that moment was all about the work you have done your entire life. That, earning that ring is not a one-season journey; it has taken a lifetime of work and dedication to get to this point. You can never imagine how it will feel until you get to experience it…and when you do, it will be better than you ever thought it would be.

Visit www.1pitchwarrior.com/extras
for BONUS 1-Pitch Warrior Tips
& FREE Systems of Success

NOTES:

NOTES:

NOTES:

CHAPTER 6: 1-PITCH WARRIOR EQUATIONS FOR SUCCESS

RATIONALIZE = RATIONAL + LIES

John Wooden said, "As long as you try your best, you are never a failure. That is, unless you blame others." There is the tendency that when things do not go our way, or we are faced with adversity, we do exactly that—blame others. We come up with lies about why we are not in the starting line-up. "Coach doesn't like me," or "coach only plays favorites," or "coach doesn't know what he is doing." We make ourselves believe them as truths. Our friends or family back us up and say the same things. We lose a game and blame the umpire for the call that he made. It is easy to do. But, it is a trap. Is your team so bad that you need every call to go your way? Do you really think that coach is out to get you? Stop lying to yourself. Accept it, deal with it, and press on. Do not dwell on it. That only brings you down along with others around you. There are two types of teammates: Fountains and Drains. Fountains lift up the team, even when things look bleak. Drains suck the life out of everyone around them by telling lies they think are true.

E + R = 0 – Event plus Response equals Outcome

When an error or a bad call occurs, you have many options on how to respond to it. You can respond to it as a 1-Pitch Warrior, or you can dwell on it, and carry the mental brick with you until your next at-bat. This is when winning takes place. It is not that the other team wins, as much as you beat yourself by focusing on the past rather than the next pitch. Remember to play against yourself. To be the best player you can be, you must master the six inches between your ears. The way you respond to events (pitches) in the course of the game, will undoubtedly play a huge part in the outcome of things. Be a 1-Pitch Warrior. Respond by saying, "So What, Next Pitch!"

RESPONSIBILITY = RESPONSE + ABILITY

Events are just that, events. We are the ones who assign meaning to them. We are the ones who must move on. We cannot limit our challenges. We must challenge our limits. You hear of the letdowns that Olympians and other champions had to go through. They describe it as disappointing, empty, and painful. They came up short long before they ever tasted the sweet taste of gold or a championship. Know that you will only get stronger by facing tough times. Just think how good it is going to feel when you prevail. When you are through changing, you are through. You have the power to respond to any situation, in either a negative way or a positive way. 1-Pitch Warriors respond the correct way and keep pressing on even when dealing with adversity.

MIND CONTROL = PERFORMANCE CONTROL

If there are 20 things running through your mind during a game, will it affect your performance? Of course, it will. "Why did I swing at that high fastball?" "Coach wants me to keep my front shoulder on the pitch." "Keep your hands inside." "Don't swing at the pitch in the dirt." "I hope he doesn't throw me that nasty curve." You get the picture. The funny thing, is we have all been there and this is not a stretch of the truth. We get analysis paralysis due to thinking about it too much. We all get close to the same results here…probably not what we want. There are exceptions, but rare. Mental toughness and being a 1-Pitch Warrior is knowing that a clear mind is much more powerful when it comes time to perform, than a fog-filled one. In this case, less is more. Being able to quiet our mind in these times is not easy. Step out of the box, off the mound, or call time—whatever you need to do to get back to the here and now. This is why recognition and routines are so important. They give an out when your mind speeds up on you. They are your go-to. They are your airbag when your mind speeds out of control, which happens to all players and coaches through most games and the season.

K – A = 0 – Knowledge minus Action equals Nothing

Your coach can give you all the knowledge he has about the game. You can read books about the game you love until your eyes are bloodshot. Watch all the DVDs available for purchase. But, without action, you will not come close to being the player that you have dreamed of becoming. It is the start that stops most people. Get going! Get going with the type of daily grind it takes to compete against the best. Action is what separates the best programs from the mediocre ones. They put in more time. It is not rocket science. Discipline and dedication fuel the fires to act on your dream and to get it done.

I – I = 0 – Information minus Inspiration equals Nothing

Playing and practicing without inspiration will get you nowhere. The one common thing you hear time and time again from champions, is the fact that they had a goal. Something was inside of them—a dream, a vision, a goal—to achieve. They also knew it was only possible by working smart and investing time in the things they knew would make them better. Never, never just go through the motions. If you just want to go through the motions, then join an aerobics class. The team is counting on everyone to get better every day. It is your responsibility to the team to put forth both mental and physical power, and to put effort into every swing, every ground ball, and every sprint. Dominate Today. Believe or Leave.

TODAY + TODAY + TODAY = YOUR LIFE

This is a simple equation to understand, but a difficult one to execute. Most people know what they need to do to get where they are going, but still fall short. Look at society. More people than ever are suffering from obesity, depression, and other issues than ever before, yet the globe is smarter than ever. Everyone wants the quick, easy fix, the simple solution. Reaching a goal is always a marathon, never a sprint. It takes small incremental changes to create excellence. Those that are average are just as close to the top as they are to the bottom. Those that separate themselves from the pack are willing to do what the average person will not. It takes courage to be different, to not merely do what everyone else is doing. It does not happen overnight. We must understand, however, that where we are today is because of the sum of our todays, and where we go in the future will be because of our right nows. Make today a masterpiece. You know what needs to be done.

BIG ENOUGH WHY = HOW

If you want to get somewhere, there is always a way to make it happen. It will not be easy. The road will have many potholes and speed bumps that will slow you down. It does not matter; get through them, or around them, or over them. Press on! Have faith that you can find a way. Nothing is impossible. Look around. The world is filled with amazing things that were not thought possible a 100 years ago. These things were just ideas, which sparked the adventure to now. If you can think big, then act big, breathe big, and commit big. If you do, your actions will produce big things.

ABOUT THE AUTHOR

Justin Dehmer's playing career started in Arizona at Shadow Mountain High School and continued into college at three different stops, including Central Arizona, where he was able to play in a JUCO World Series and become an Academic All-American. From there, Dehmer played at Kansas State University and Grand Canyon University. Once in Iowa, Dehmer jumped right into the coaching ranks as the Assistant Varsity Coach at Earlham High School for two years and then as the Head Coach for two more years before landing the job at Martensdale-St. Mary's for five more years. He boasts an impressive 203-48 (.829) winning record and was selected as the Coach of the Year in 2010, 2011, and 2012. His team was nationally recognized for their 88-game winning streak, which is the 2nd best ever in high school baseball. After winning back-to-back-to-back State Championships in 2010 (43-0), 2011 (44-0), 2012 (40-5), Coach Dehmer left coaching high school baseball to invest in what means more to him than any championship, his family. He continues to teach high school math at Southeast Polk and resides in Norwalk, Iowa where his wife Angie is a realtor and their two children, daughter Grace, 6 and son Gavin, 5 go to school. He continues to stay close to the game as a clinic speaker, writing books/articles for baseball publications, and consulting for both high school and college programs about the mental game and planning for excellence with the 1-Pitch Warrior System.

NOTES:

www.1pitchwarrior.com

NOTES:

1-PITCH WARRIOR SYSTEM

- 45-MINUTE HITTING VIDEO

- 90 1-PW PRESENTATION VIDEO

- PITCHING PROCESS AUDIO

- 1-PW AUDIO

- ANATOMY OF A WINNING STREAK AUDIO

- INTERVIEW WITH BRIAN CAIN

- MENTAL TOUGHNESS AUDIOS

- 1-PW DOCUMENTS AND FILES

A $200+ VALUE FOR ONLY $99

GO TO www1PitchWarrior.com

TO ORDER

WHO IS BRIAN CAIN?

About The Master of The Mental Game

Brian M. Cain, MS, CMAA, is the #1 best selling author of Toilets, Bricks Fish Hooks and PRIDE: The Peak Performance Toolbox EXPOSED, So What, Next Pitch!, and The Mental Conditioning Manual. A leading authority and expert in the area of Mental Conditioning, Peak Performance Coaching, and Applied Sport Psychology, Cain has worked with coaches, athletes, and teams at the Olympic level and in the National Football League (NFL), National Basketball Association (NBA), National Hockey League (NHL), Ultimate Fighting Championship (UFC), and Major League Baseball (MLB) on using mental conditioning to perform at their best when it means the most.

Cain has also worked with programs in some of the top college athletic departments around the country, including the University of Alabama, Auburn University, Florida State University, the

University of Iowa, the University of Maryland, the University of Mississippi, Mississippi State University, Oregon State University, the University of Southern California, the University of Tennessee, Texas Christian University, Vanderbilt University, Washington State University, Yale University, and many others.

Cain has worked as a mental-conditioning consultant with numerous high school, state, and national-championship programs. He has delivered his award-winning seminars and presentations at coaches' clinics, leadership summits, and athletic directors' conventions all over the country. As a high-school athletic director, he is one of the youngest ever to receive the Certified Master Athletic Administration Certification from the National Interscholastic Athletic Administrator's Association.

A highly-sought-after Peak Performance Coach, clinician, and keynote and motivational speaker, Cain delivers his message with passion, enthusiasm, and in an engaging style that keeps his audiences entertained while being educated. As someone who lives what he teaches, Cain will inspire you and give you the tools necessary to get the most out of your career.

Find out when Cain will be coming to your area by visiting his calendar at **www.briancain.com.**

How Can You Become a Master
of the Mental Game:

Discover What The Inner Circle Delivers

If you're a serious coach or athlete looking to take your performance to another level, I highly encourage you to join the Brian Cain Peak Performance Inner Circle. Lifetime members receive interviews with top coaches and athletes, videos of top performance routines, and inside access to Cain and his teachings. The Brian Cain Peak Performance Inner Circle will help you play at your best when it means the most. Go online to **www.briancaininnercircle.com** to sign up today.

THE PEAK PERFORMANCE SYSTEM
P.R.I.D.E. – Personal Responsibility
In Daily Excellence

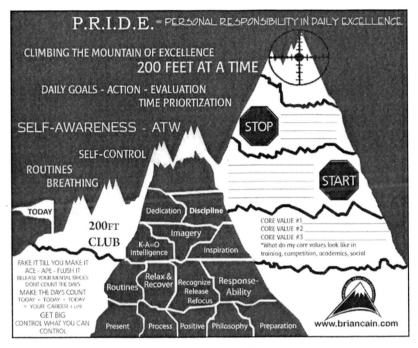

Have You or Your Team Ever Struggled With...

- Working hard physically but **still not getting the results you deserve?**

- Creating a system to **teach character and toughness** that translates to the field?

- **Investing time and money into books, videos and programs** that don't get results?

- Repeatedly **getting it done in practice, but failing to do so when the lights come on?**

- **Choking in pressure situations** time after time, even though you have been there before?

The Peak-Performance System Will...

- Give you the best step-by-step system ever created for developing mental toughness.

- Teach you the same mental-toughness system used by world-champion athletes.

- Be the equivalent of having the **world's best strength and conditioning coach...for your brain.**

- Positively **change your athletic and coaching career.**

- **Unlock your potential** and teach you how to be your best every day.

Cain's Peak Performance System (PRIDE – Personal Responsibility In Daily Excellence) is a 6-DVD Peak Performance training program, featuring eighteen 10-25 minute videos and a 100+ page manual designed for the coach or athlete looking to gain a competitive advantage from Peak-Performance and Mental-Toughness Training. Cain goes in-depth on the following topics:

1. The Language of Mental Toughness

2. 200-FT Club & Core Covenants

3. Present-Moment Focus

4. Process-Over-Outcome Approaches

5. Championship Perspective

6. Positive Mental Attitudes

7. Preparation Routines for Confidence

8. Preparation Routines for Consistent Performance

9. RESPONSE-Ability Training

10. In-depth Relaxation & Recovery Training

11. Performance-Awareness Development

12. K-A=O – The Intelligence Factor

13. Mental-Imagery Training

14. Inspiration & Motivation that Works

15. Dedication & Commitment

16. Discipline as a Positive Life Skill

17. Excellence as a Lifestyle, Not an Event

18. Interview with an MMA World Champion

Visit www.briancain.com/cainproducts/pride/

For A Sneak Peak of The Peak Performance System In Action

THE PEAK PERFORMANCE BOOTCAMP

CAIN'S LIVE FOUR-HOUR SEMINAR
2 DVDS, 3 AUDIO CDS, MANUAL

Have You or Your Team Ever Struggled With...

- The ability to *sustain consistently high levels of performance?*

- *Getting distracted* by a large crowd, hostile environment or "BIG GAME?"

- Finding ways to keep your team *motivated to work HARD & SMART everyday?*

- Ways to *make practice more competitive* and intense?

- *Choking in pressure situations* time after time even though you have been there before?

Today You Can Discover How To Help Your Team:

- Gain the mental toughness they need to *out-play and out-perform* even the toughest competition.

- *Play in the moment* and destroy all those mental blocks that kill performance.

- Take control over the speed and the flow of the game so all the competition is *playing at your pace.*

- Shatter their beliefs about what they "cannot do."

- Give them the tools *to accomplish things they once only dreamed of.*

- Develop the *team chemistry* you need to bring home a championship.

For A Sneak Peak of The PRIDE Peak Performance Bootcamp visit www.briancain.com/cainproducts/bootcamp

Have You or Your Team Ever Struggled With...

- Consistently *playing at your best?*

- Finding the motivation it takes to *work hard every day?*

- Maintaining *confidence* when you are *not playing well?*

- Choking in pressure situations *time after time* even though you have been there before?

The Introduction To Peak Performance CD Will...

- Give you insight into the *fundamentals of peak performance.*

- Help you to become a *Master of The Mental Game.*

- Increase your *ability to overcome adversity.*

- Teach you the psychological skills necessary to *perform consistently at your best.*

"This CD lives in my car's CD player. Cain breaks down the fundamental aspects of mental toughness and gives you the skills necessary to teach toughness to your team. Every coach and athlete should have this CD in their car or on their iPod at all times."

Eric Bakich
Head Baseball Coach
University of Michigan

At the elite levels, athletic performance is 90% mental and 10% physical.

In this CD you get the information you need to perform your best when it means the most.

You get the tactics, the training, and the secrets you need to increase your mental toughness.

You get you the tools that will put your mental game MILES AHEAD of every other athlete and team in your league, in your conference, or in your division.

That is exactly why I created this CD... so that YOU can discover:

- Why sport psychology and *peak performance is crucial* to your success this season!

- The tricks and methods that teach you how to *let go of the things you cannot control* during play!

- The *3 "magic letters"* that turn statements of failure into goal-setting exclamations!

- How to make *excellence a LIFESTYLE* and not a once-in-a-while event!

- The little secrets that allow you to *increase your ability to play at a quicker tempo!*

- The right way – *and the wrong way – to talk on defense!*

"I started using this CD when I met Cain and it has helped me be a better fighter, a better coach, more mentally tough, and more confident. Learning to focus on the things I can control, learning that confidence is a choice, learning not to count the days but to make the days count has had a tremendous impact on my career. Cain covers all of this and his P.R.I.D.E. program in this CD. I cannot recommend this CD any more highly to the coach or athlete looking to increase his performance with mental toughness training."

Rob MacDonald
Professional Mixed Martial Arts Fighter, UFC
Strength and Conditioning Coach, Gym Jones

Visit www.BrianCain.com/products
for more information

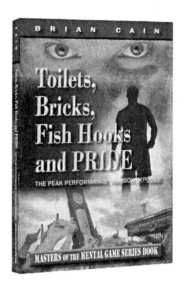

Featured on ESPN

Have you ever experienced any of the following?

- Continually *falling short of your potential?*
- *Mental game breakdowns* under pressure?
- Coaches or athletes who simply are *not as motivated as you?*
- Wasting time thinking about things you have *no control over?*
- *Losing to an inferior opponent* more than once in a season
- Wanting to quit because you *lost the love?*
- Coaches that make a simple sport *more complex than it needs to be?*

Visit www.ToiletsBricksFishHooksandPride.com
For FREE Extras, Updates & Information

SO WHAT, NEXT PITCH!
How To Play Your Best
When It Means The Most
Book Two in the Series

SO WHAT, NEXT PITCH! WILL:

- Give you a system for playing the game one pitch at a time

- Take you inside some of the best minds in the game of baseball

- Show you how to deal with failure both on the field and in life

- Serve as your map on the journey to mental toughness

- Unlock your potential and give you the mental keys to success

"This book will make a difference in the way you compete in baseball, but more importantly, the way you compete at the game of life."

Dave Serrano, Head Baseball Coach
The University of Tennessee

"Moving on to the next pitch is easier said than done. This book will show you how to do it."

Gary Gilmore, Head Baseball Coach
Coastal Carolina University
2012 Big South Conference Champions
& 2012 Big South Coach of The Year

"So What, Next Pitch! It is something that you hear all the time in baseball. In this book you learn some strategies that will help you play the game one pitch at a time and overcome the failure that is part of the game."

Trevor Moawad, MAT, Director of Performance
IMG Academies

Visit www.SoWhatNextPitch.com For
BONUS Mental Conditioning Material
& Peak Performance Training Tools

The Mental Conditioning Manual:
Your Blueprint For Excellence

www.1pitchwarrior.com

This book gives you the exact system Cain uses to build champions and masters of the mental game. This is the same system that has produced five mixed martial arts world champions, NCAA National Champions and High School State and National Champions. Now, YOU can use Cain's system to unlock your potential and play your best when it means the most.

Cain's #1 Bestselling Book *Toilets, Bricks, Fish Hooks and PRIDE: The Peak Performance Toolbox EXPOSED*, sold over 3,200 copies in its first 32 days and was featured on ESPN during The University of Alabama Softball team's 2012 NCAA National Championship run. *The Mental Conditioning Manual* gives you the detailed system that Cain shares with his top performing clients. You can unlock your potential so you can DOMINATE the day, everyday!

"The secrets of success are in your hands. The Mental Conditioning Manual is a breakthrough in peak performance and personal development. This is your blueprint for making excellence a lifestyle, not an event."

Jim Schlossnagle, Head Baseball Coach, TCU
04, 05, 06, 07, 08, 09, 10, 11, 12 Conference Champions
2010 Men's College World Series
2010 National College Baseball Coach of The Year
2013 Team USA National Baseball Team Head Coach

"This book is the foundation of our program's mental conditioning program. Cain keeps simplifying the process and making it easier to train the six inches between the ears that control the six feet below. This is a must-have for any coach or player."

Vann Studeman, Head Softball Coach
Mississippi State University

"This is one of the only books I take with me when I leave the house for spring training. It has everything I need to keep me focused on the process and what I need to do to play my best."

Andrew Cashner, San Diego Padres, Pitcher
2008 1st Round Pick, Chicago Cubs

"Cain is the Master of the Mental Game. He helps you to keep yourself focused on the right things to help your performance. The Mental Conditioning Manual is a key part of my routine."

Bryan Holaday, Detroit Tigers, Catcher
2010 Johnny Bench Award For Top Catcher In College Baseball

"Playing the game one pitch at a time is a critical part of success in baseball. Living your life one pitch at a time is also the best way to accomplish your goals off the field. What I love most about The Mental Conditioning Manual is the amount of information you can get in one place. For high school and college athletes, this book is a must.

What Cain does is give you a system for communicating and teaching more effectively about competitiveness, mental toughness and the skills athletes need to succeed in college football and in life. His program made a huge difference in our 2010 Big South championship season."

David Bennett, Former Head Football Coach
Coastal Carolina University, 2010 Big South Champions

THE MENTAL CONDITIONING MANUAL WILL TRAIN YOU TO:

- Live in the present moment and maximize your time

- Act different than how you feel

- Start having good "bad" days

- Focus on the process over the outcome

- Identify what you can control and what you cannot

- Create a personal philosophy and core values for your life

- Challenge your limiting beliefs and your perspective

- Stay positive in the face of adversity

- Establish performance routines for consistency

- Take responsibility for your performance and life

- Gain control of your thoughts, feelings, and emotions

- Develop the performance awareness needed to win

- Release negative thoughts and negative energy

- Use mental imagery to boost your confidence

- Motivate yourself to make the impossible possible

- Have the dedication and self-discipline needed for success

Visit www.TheMentalConditioningManual.com For

"So What, Next Pitch! It is something that you hear all the time in baseball. In this book you learn some strategies that will help you to play the game one pitch at a time and overcome the failure that is part of the game."

Trevor Moawad, MAT, Director of Performance
IMG Academies

"Baseball is a mental game. Brian Cain is a Master of The Mental Game and in So What, Next Pitch!, he outlines what a coach and player should be doing to give themselves the best chance for success."

Steve Smith, Head Baseball Coach, Baylor University
2012 Big XII Conference Champions
& 2012 Big XII Coach of The Year

"Cain was a graduate student assistant at Cal State Fullerton in 2002-2003 and he established himself as a hard worker who was only going to have success. In this book, So What, Next Pitch!, he has outlined what it takes to be a champion of the mental game and what it takes to play this game between the ears at the highest level. All of our players at Cal State Fullerton will read it, and more importantly, will work to put the concepts into daily practice."

Rick Vanderhook, Head Baseball Coach, Cal State Fullerton
2012 Big West Conference Champions
& 2012 Big West Coach of The Year

CONNECT WITH CAIN
THROUGH SOCIAL MEDIA
YOUR LINK TO DOING A LITTLE A LOT, NOT A LOT A LITTLE

 www.twitter.com/briancainpeak

 www.facebook.com/briancainpeak

 www.linkedin.com/briancainpeak

 www.youtube.com/wwwbriancaincom

 www.briancain.com/itunes

SIGN UP FOR YOUR FREE NEWSLETTER
www.BrianCain.com